THE CRY OF A

Pastor

DR. HURDIS BOZEMAN

TRILOGY
PROFESSIONAL PUBLISHING MEETS POWERFUL PROMOTION

A wholly owned subsidary of **TBN**

The Cry of a Pastor

Trilogy Christian Publishers A Wholly Owned Subsidiary of Trinity Broadcasting Network

2442 Michelle Drive Tustin, CA 92780

Rights Department, 2442 Michelle Drive, Tustin, CA 92780.

Trilogy Christian Publishing/TBN and colophon are trademarks of Trinity Broadcasting Network.

For information about special discounts for bulk purchases, please contact Trilogy Christian Publishing.

Trilogy Disclaimer: The views and content expressed in this book are those of the author and may not necessarily reflect the views and doctrine of Trilogy Christian Publishing or the Trinity Broadcasting Network.

Manufactured in the United States of America

10 9 8 7 6 5 4 3 2 1

Library of Congress Cataloging-in-Publication Data is available.

ISBN: 978-1-68556-757-6

E-ISBN: 978-1-68556-758-3

DEDICATION

This book is dedicated to:

The late Bishop Frank T. Bozeman

Mrs. Twanna Brown, editor

Dr. J. C. and Mother Ella Wade, Jr.

Dr. Walter E. and First Lady Sadie Ellis

Pastor James and First Lady Cynthia Mctier, Jr.

Senior Pastor Colenthia Milner (David) Wright

Rev. Fagale Shuford-Grant

Mrs. Marlene Joyce (Jesse) Hall

Pastor Michele Milner-Copeland

Rev. Humphrey L. (Mrs. Linda) Shuford

Dr. James W. Shuford

Dr. Claude A. (Rev. Brenda) Shuford

Rev. Robert L. (Sister Anna) Shuford

Elder Charles (Kenosha) Shuford

Mr. Steve (Rose) Smith

Mrs. Becky (Sonny) Jackson

Mrs. Mary (Issac) McQueen

Mr. Bobby (Precious) Smith

Pastor Alice Milner-Gipson

Chaplain Beth McDaniel-Rogers

Minister Felecia (Deacon James) McBride

Nieces and nephews

ACKNOWLEDGMENTS

In loving memory:

Bishop Frank T. Bozeman

Deacon Willie Lee Milner

Pastor Charlena Kay Shuford-Miller

Percival Ann Shuford

Loretta Karen Shuford

Diane Smith

Rev. Cora Rebecca Crenshaw-Shuford

Mr. Robert Lee Shuford

Rev. David Lee Grant

Rev. Dan (Maxie) Johnson

Willie Lee Milner, Jr.

Larry Danyell Milner

Deacon Roscoe George

Sister Jettie George

Mother Irene Milner

Mr. Jeremiah Milner, Sr.

Rev. Wilbert and Sister Deloris Milner, Sr.

Deacon C. B. and Cora Jean Milner, Sr.

Pastor Douglas L. Nicholson, Sr.

(the pastor who licensed and ordained me)

Evangelist Sarah Nell Marshall

Philip Samone Williams

Aunties and uncles

CONTENTS

FOREWORD

Bishop, Dr. Hurdis Shuford-Bozeman has been given divine instructions and revelation knowledge, and she is a blessing to the body of Christ. She is a blessing to pastors, leaders, and laity in her community and in the nation. Therefore, she is a living testimony of faith, endurance, life changes, and life challenges. Hurdis is the first Black female pastor to be licensed, ordained as a pastor, and build a National Baptist Convention, USA, Inc., church in her region. Furthermore, she was a pastor in the National Baptist Convention, USA, Inc., when God gave her the assignment to pastor the Good Hope Missionary Baptist Church, Wetumpka, Alabama, in 2000. Moreover, Bishop Bozeman has made history, and she is a trailblazer for women in ministry in the region where she resides.

She is an excellent example of the virtuous woman in Proverbs, chapter thirty-one. Also, she is a woman of God with great reverence for God, her spiritual leaders, and her God-given kingdom assignment. Hurdis has integrity, perseverance, purpose, tenacity, and a passion for Christ Jesus. She has been in ministry for thirty-eight years as a licensed and ordained preacher of the gospel of our Lord and Savior, Jesus Christ. In like manner, Hurdis was Elmore Rehoboth district's missionary of the association for fifteen years.

She was a public school teacher in the Macon County public school system and a leader in the district youth organization. Hurdis has served as a youth minister, assistant pastor, and pastor, and she is serving as the first female presiding bishop of Global Word Fellowship, Inc., Montgomery, Alabama.

Hurdis has weathered many storms of life, and she is qualified to write this book, *The Cry of a Pastor*. In her book, she will share testimonies of faith and her personal life experiences.

In closing: the storms, the trials, the tribulations, and the achievements in ministry have given Bishop Hurdis Bozeman a greater appreciation of her kingdom assignments. She has a greater passion for God and her fellow man. This book will empower you and bless you richly.

The late Bishop Frank T. Bozeman

CHAPTER 1

The Pastor after God's Own Heart

Yes, Lord Jesus, I am so glad that You are our provider, our deliverer, our sustainer of life, our peace, our healer, and our Savior. You continuously load Your children with daily benefits.

Pastors, we have a blessed, glorious, magnificent, and almighty God. He can do all things, exceedingly and abundantly, above more than we can ask or think. What do you do, pastors and leaders, when life takes you in a different direction? How do you handle your position as a pastor or a leader when it's too difficult to explain to others? Yes, these questions are very important to pastors and leaders. There are times when pastors will encounter some very difficult life changes and major challenges. Sometimes, life changes will cause you to ask questions, be overwhelmed, and question your God-given plans.

However, when you ask God some of these life-changing questions, you may not get the answers that you want to hear. God's answers may be: "Wait and do not get weary in well-doing." He may say, "Be still and know that I am

God." He may say no, or He may say it's not your battle and to take your hands off the situation. When God gives the answers, we have to trust Him for the final results. Moreover, when you have inclined your ears to hear from God and receive His answers, it can be overwhelming if you allow your flesh to override the Holy Spirit. You may cry out in anger and dismay, but, pastors, better days will come to you.

His answers come with protection and provision. You must follow Jesus's instructions. In like manner, you have to continue trusting and seeking Jesus so you can hear His voice clearly and precisely. When Jesus speaks, you must be ready and willing to follow His guidance and His directions. However, after you have heard Jesus's voice and His word, you must receive the word and obey it.

"Obedience is better than sacrifice" (1 Samuel 15:22, DARBY). Therefore, all pastors and leaders should obey God if they are going to lead His people. Moses obeyed God and led the children of Israel out of Egypt. Egypt was a place of difficulty, bondage, pain, and much suffering for God's people. Moses was a pastor, a prophet, an under-shepherd, and a servant called by God. He had to lead His people out of slavery. The Word of God tells us in Jeremiah 3:15 (NIV): "Then I will give you shepherds after my own heart, who will lead you with knowledge and understanding."

God's servant, Moses, was a "leader of leaders" and a man chosen by God for the ministry of leadership. His job was not easy, nor was it safe during his ministry, but God always protected Moses. However, Moses had an assignment that was difficult, distracting, disappointing, rough, and sometimes very tough. Some of Moses's days were distracting, as so many pastors' days are now. During this pandemic, some pastors have had to encounter life-threatening dangers as Moses did. Moses had some good days, draining days, disgusting days, and some victorious days. On the other hand, Moses also had some days of breakthroughs and deliverance. He was a conqueror and a deliverer for the children of Israel.

Moses helped God's people, day after day, face various situations. During Moses's tenure as a servant leader, Moses stood for righteousness. He fell but got back up and continued his assignment.

I may go through some days of testing and trials, but I will stand for Jesus for the rest of my life. I am His servant leader, the late Bishop Frank T., and Bishop Hurdis Shuford-Bozeman—the end-time harvest leader.

Moses was one of God's chosen leaders. Therefore, pastors and leaders must obey God and lead by example. Pastors must keep Jesus Christ as their role model and His principles as their guide. Jesus Christ is the Great Shepherd of all sheep. He is our everlasting Father. Pastors, we must trust Him.

Likewise, as pastors and leaders, you have to follow the Great Shepherd and keep leading as an undershepherd. You must lead in difficult times, jubilant times, and in times of crisis. Our Lord and Savior, Jesus the Christ, the Anointed One, led His disciples in a time of crisis and conflict.

Jesus is the pastor of all pastors. Jesus is the protection for the sheep, the guide, the doctor, the provider for the sheep, and He is more than enough. The Bible says that He is our "all in all" (1 Corinthians 15:28, NIV). The pastor after God's own heart has a strong determination to fight for the sheep, care for them, love them, give them guidance, share with them, and correct them. Without God's love, grace, mercy, forgiveness, restoration, giving, and faith-dedicated pastors and leaders, it would be no one shepherding the sheep. Pastors after God's own heart know that it's all about Jesus working through them for the good of God's people. Whatever you need, God has it. He is ready to give you His best. Pastors and leaders must have the heart of Jesus; their minds must be like Jesus Christ's. "Let this mind be in you which was also in Christ Jesus" (Philippians 2:5, NKJV).

When Jesus ordains His pastors and leaders, He gives them a heart for His people. Jesus will also equip, settle, establish, and make you perfect in Him. He is the true vine, and we are the branches (John 15:1). He is the one with divine pruning skills and branch-building abilities.

Today, there are some pastors all over the world giving the sheep the best that they have, and they are not appreciated. They are sold out, real, loyal, devoted, dependable, dedicated, and soldiers in the army of Jesus. The real pastors are not going to compromise; they will stay rooted and grounded in Jesus Christ. In like manner, they will encourage, empower, uplift, and embrace other leaders and the sheep. Therefore, all real pastors must continue to seek God's advice and His help, pray the prayer of faith, and pray for the sheep to advance in the things of God.

Noah Manyika calls pastors "servant leaders." Will all the "servant leaders" continue to cry out to Jesus for your family, your sheep, this nation, and this world? We are in a pandemic, but Jesus is faithful.

The Servant Leaders' Prayer

Dear Jesus, I am coming to You again with thanksgiving and supplication. My heart and the hearts of some of the other pastors are heavy, but today, Jesus, we will not pray about the pandemic. We shall pray a prayer of thanksgiving and intercession. We thank You, Jesus, for all the undershepherds abiding in the nations throughout the world. Jesus, they are Your chosen vessels, divinely called and chosen by You. Dear Jesus, thank You for carrying them from glory to glory and from strength to strength. These pastors are God's instruments of love, peace, and guidance. Thank You for giving them Your peace like that of a river. Thank You for giving them Your joy, unspeakable, full of glory, Your understanding, Your wisdom, and Your knowledge. Jesus, thank You for giving them the wisdom to lead their flock correctly, with confidence and courage. Thank You, Jesus, for encouraging pastors and giving them Your divine counsel.

We thank You, Jesus, for blessing all Your pastors as Your "servant leaders." Heavenly Father, we decree and declare that pastors are protected by Your angels. They are covered with the blood of Jesus. The pastors are praying, proclaiming Your Word, speaking the name of Jesus, and pleading the blood of Jesus. They are ministers of Your righteousness, and they are kingdom builders. When pastors pray, Jesus, will You allow the power of the Holy Ghost to fall afresh on them? Jesus, will You continue to allow the mighty wind of the Holy Ghost to breathe fresh fire on them? Jesus, will You continue to allow them to preach and teach with power, prophetic power, clarity, and conviction?

Thank You, Jesus: Your pastors are winning souls, bringing restoration, salvation, healing, and deliverance. Hallelujah, hallelujah, hallelujah! Moreover, Jesus, we thank You for their families and their church families working together in unity. Thank You, Jesus, that their families and church families are covered with Your blood. Thank You that their finances are increasing because they have given their tithes and offerings. Your increase is empowering them right now to continue to be a blessing to others.

We thank You, Jesus, that they are the lenders and not the borrowers, that they are the head and not the tail, that they are above only and not beneath; the blessings of the Lord are overtaking them now. In Jesus's mighty name, amen.

Saints, the pastoral role takes a strong level of commitment, sacrifice, and obedience on behalf of the undershepherds. Jesus was the greatest of all pastors. He was the pastor of His twelve disciples and many more sheep. During His earthly ministry, Jesus taught them; He prayed for them; He disciplined and guided them. He healed them, and He gave them unconditional love.

Surely, as pastors, you are giving the sheep what is required of the undershepherds. The flock must follow the pastor, and the pastor must lead by the precepts and examples of Jesus. Jesus is the Lord of lords and the King of kings. Pastors, you must have faith and confidence; you are in a position of authority, assurance, and power. Keep the faith and always trust Jesus for everything. The pastor has authority and assurance because of their connection with Jesus, the Chief Cornerstone, the Great I Am, the Lily of the Valley, and the Bridge over troubled waters. Jesus has trusted His pastors to take charge of His sheep to lead, teach, and guide them. He has given the pastors "the greater works" to do (John 14:12, NKJV). Pastors impart to the sheep and feed them with spiritual food. Also, pastors have the confidence to decree profound, prophetic, and powerful biblical doctrines to their sheep.

"The race is not given to the swift nor the strong, but to those who will endure to the end."[1] Jesus endured the cross, took the sins of the world, and defeated death, hell, and the grave. He rose with all power in His hands. Pastors, you can make it with Jesus; Jesus's got you. Jesus is the divine prophet, the apostle, the pastor, the evangelist, and the teacher in the fivefold ministry. He is the ultimate example. We must follow His examples and teachings and use His methods with total confidence. He is our redeemer, the King of kings, our provider, and our healer. He is everything that we need.

Pastors, again, I say to you: trust Jesus for everything. As for my house and me, we have kept the faith and cried out to Jesus day and night. Jesus is our midnight rider, and He is our keeper. I had to stand among wolves and proclaim Jesus to the masses. There were members, pastors, leaders, and some in my family who did not believe in women preachers. There were so many days that I cried, "Lord, have mercy!"—a pastor's cry. Sometimes it is a silent cry. But when you are crying and need a role model, you can look to Jesus. He is the best role model in the world.

I have used His guidance and wisdom over and over again. He has laid the pastoral foundation for all pastors: they can follow Him and won't miss a beat. The men and women of God and leaders can follow Jesus with faith and trust twenty-four seven and always get assured results. He will make you "fishermen of men" and the best undershepherds in town. Trust Him with your life.

Again, I say: Pastors, what do you do when you don't know what to do? There are times when pastors are faced with difficult problems. When you don't know what to do, Jesus will give you the right answers. You can go to the rock; Jesus is the rock. Those pastors with the heart of God will find the answers in God's Word. There are answers in the Word of God for every situation that you will ever face or encounter.

"Man shall not live by bread alone, but by every word that proceedeth out of the mouth of God" (Matthew 4:4). The Word of God is: "A lamp unto my feet, and a light unto my path" (Psalm 119:105). Therefore, pastors must let the Word of God lead them to the truth and keep on moving forward.

"Thy word have I hid in my heart that I might not sin against thee" (Psalm 119:11, DARBY). The undershepherds who are called after God's own heart cannot be bound by traditions, legalism, and secular opinions. They will abide by the Word of God. Pastors must stay rooted and grounded in the Word of God. They must be led by the spirit of God if they are the sons of God. Romans 8:14 (NKJV) says, "For as many as are led by the Spirit of God, these are sons of God." Women and men are included here as "sons of God"; they are "servant leaders." In Jesus's spiritual order, there is no gender. In like manner, female pastors are not an afterthought; they are "sons of God," and they are called to His kingdom assignments.

God made woman when He made man; woman was taken out of man. He made woman, and He has called some of His women to a pastoral ministry. He has given women leadership positions in church and in the secular arena. Who did it? God did it in His divine way. Saints, remember to read the Word of God and get understanding.

Also, read the profound book *Why Can't Women Preach?* by Dr. Frank T. Bozeman. In his book, he gives revelation knowledge and biblical truth concerning women in ministry. He is an apologetic. Yes, he is a prophetic defender of the faith. It is a must-read, and you will be blessed beyond measure.

The women in ministry who I am connected to are pastoring with power and operating in the Holy Ghost. They are powerful, profound, and prosperous women of God. Women must praise Jesus right now for all His love and benefits that He has bestowed upon them. Again, I say: Jesus has no gender in the spirit. He is using men, women, boys, and girls in various areas of ministry all around the world. Jesus has used me as a minister, servant leader, and pastor for thirty-seven years. Moreover, He empowered me as a youth speaker when I was sixteen years old. Also, my mother had me do recitations and sing at a very young age. She instilled in all her children much wisdom, the Word of God, the love of God, education, good workmanship, high morals, respect for themselves and others, as well as good survival skills. Yes, our mother, late Rev. Cora Rebecca Crenshaw-Shuford, was a preacher, teacher, and exhorter of the Word. Thank You, Jesus, for our dear mother and our awesome and loving dad.

Furthermore, in August 2021, I will celebrate thirty-seven years in ministry, and my husband, Bishop Frank T. Bozeman, will celebrate forty-three years in ministry. I was chosen as a servant and a leader by Jesus. The women pastors are called, chosen, and empowered by God to do kingdom work. We want to hear Jesus say, "Well done."

When Jesus sees you, He sees the image of Him. We all are "fearfully and wonderfully made" (Psalm 139:14, NIV). Jesus wants you to let His light and love shine through you. The Bible says, "Let your light so shine before men, that they may see your good works, and glorify your Father which is in heaven" (Matthew 5:16).

The pastors after God's own heart are chosen to serve Jesus's sheep. They are His workmanship, created in Christ Jesus (Ephesians 2:10). The walk of pastors and the talk of pastors should line up with Jesus's Word. There will be days when pastors have to pray, cry, forgive, love, bury the dead, marry the couples, smile, and bring the Word on the same day. Pastors are human: they hurt; they get wounded, but they still stand for Jesus. They will encounter some weapons, but these shall not prosper (Isaiah 54:17).

The pastors after God's own heart have to minister to their family, friends, church members, coworkers, supervisors, and other individuals. The family of the pastor is their first ministry. The Holy Spirit reveals to them their spiritual assignments. "Charity begins at home, and then charity is shared abroad." When the ministry and the pastor are under attack, the family is under attack. "Many are the afflictions of the righteous; but God shall deliver them out of them all" (Psalm 34:19).

Again, pastors are human. There will be days when they have to take some time off to pray and consecrate themselves. The members will not always understand, agree, help, pray, follow, obey, or minister to the pastor. But pastors have to continue doing the work of the ministry until Jesus says, "Well done." Oh yes, pastors must have some time off for vacations, sabbaticals, and relaxing days.

Furthermore, there are times when pastors are hurting, and they still have to minister out of their hurt and brokenness. The Holy Spirit is their healer, helper, deliverer, guide, and comforter.

Pastors will have to fast and pray to win victories and become more than conquerors on this journey of faith. Some victories will be won only by fasting and praying. The Bible says, "Howbeit this kind goeth not out but by prayer and fasting" (Matthew 17:21). The pastors after God's own heart will go forth powerfully, in the mighty name of Jesus!

CHAPTER 2

God's Favor

The favor of the Lord is upon you, pastors: God has anointed you to preach the gospel. What does "favor" mean to you? The word "favor" means: "to be in support," "to the advantage of," "preferential treatment," "to prefer," or "approval." I say that favor is God's grace and that it is sufficient for you. Pastors may not deserve His grace, but it is His unmerited favor to His people. Thank You, God, for Your favor.

The pastor's sheep don't always understand the favor that God has released on the undershepherd. The sheep are blind and have to be led by the undershepherd. The Great Shepherd has to lead the pastor. However, sometimes a sheep wants to lead the undershepherd, and this is not God's perfect will, nor is it His way. Moreover, when a sheep tries to lead other sheep, the blind are leading the blind. In the Bible, Aaron and Miriam rose against Moses, and Miriam was struck with leprosy. The Bible says when the blind lead the blind, they will fall in a ditch (Matthew 15:14). Saints need to stay in the position that God has assigned to them.

The favor and the spiritual authority that pastors are given come from God. They are for the building of His kingdom. They are not given to pastors to be used against others, nor are they given for vainglory. Pastors are called and chosen by God. They are chosen after God's own heart. He will give them the instructions for His sheep. The favor of leadership is upon them as God's chosen servant leaders.

Pastors chosen after the heart of God will hear God's instruction and will walk in His favor. Therefore, those who are true pastors will focus on God's purposes and His plans for the ministry. The favor of God will be released in their lives, and they will walk in obedience, not in rebellion. Yes, sometimes, they may fall in different areas, but they must get up, repent, and move forward in Jesus's perfect will. His grace is sufficient for them, and His strength is made perfect in every weakness (2 Corinthians 12:9).

When pastors are in a position that God has given them, they will wait on their promotions and new opportunities. Yes, there are days they may miss the mark, but the Holy Spirit will draw them back to God.

It is good when members and others stay out of God's way when He is correcting the undershepherd. There are some assignments given to the sheep to complete, but there are others that the sheep have to let God handle. The pastor is human and not divine. Jesus came to the earth as God and man, human and divine. God's favor is on pastors, and He will usher them into His divine order. This is a great time for God's promises, perfection, order, government, and divine alignment.

Pastors are human and not divine.

Jesus is human and divine.

However, some of the sheep look to their pastor as their god or their great and divine shepherd. Pastors are undershepherds; they are soldiers in God's army. Sometimes, they get wounded in the army, and they need to be healed. Saints, give pastors the time to heal. Pastors have to take care of themselves too. They are workmen in the vineyard, rightly dividing the word of truth. The Bible says, "The laborer is worthy of his hire" (Luke 10:7). Pastors also need to rest. The things that the sheep can take care of should be completed by them. Saints, give pastors the time to complete God's work and live their lives according to the Word of God. Pastors desire to have time to pray, study, laugh, and meditate. They need the time to minister and love their families. Pastors need encouragement and need real, genuine support.

Pastors have God's favor; they have to wait on God before moving with His plans. Saints, stop rushing your pastors into your agendas. "But those who wait on the LORD shall renew their strength, they shall mount up with the wings of eagles, they shall run and not be weary, they shall walk and not faint" (Isaiah 40:31, NKJV).

Furthermore, let's continue to pray for God's pastors across the nations. They are called and chosen by God to feed the flock of God. They are called to give divine instructions, wisdom, knowledge, understanding, and revelations from God. Pastors also give spiritual guidance and much more. Therefore, pastors have to win souls for Christ, build them up in Christ, and send them out for Christ. It takes time, resources, and finances to build the kingdom. When pastors continue to labor with the sheep, they will see the advancement of God's kingdom.

Spending quality time in prayer will produce God's divine favor, faith, and love. So, the place for pastors to work is the position that God has assigned them in the earth realm. Deacons, deaconesses, missionaries, and members should go and get the sheep. The world is filled with unsaved souls. Saints must stop putting the burdens and all the responsibilities of the ministry on pastors. Pastors have to work where God has called them. We have to delegate assignments to individuals with the ministry gifts and calling of various ministries.

What a blessing it has been in our ministry to see those chosen and called by God working in their areas of ministry! When God shows us the people to use in the ministry, we are guided by the Holy Spirit to appoint them without regrets. Yes, training has to be implemented, as well as fasting, prayer, mentorship, and correcting when it's necessary and in order. Ministers and members have to be mentored, encouraged, taught, and given guidance during training. This is a vital part of pastoral leadership.

Sometimes, people in the sheepfold may exhibit the Judas spirit to help them. When this spirit is present, you can expect discord and betrayal in the like manner that Jesus had one disciple who betrayed Him. This disciple's name was Judas Iscariot. Not everyone will be like Judas. Moreover, as pastors, we cannot get discouraged when we find a Judas in the camp. We must seek Jesus for guidance and follow Jesus's directions quickly.

Moses, the servant leader, found out during his pastoral leadership that he needed help. Oh yes, Moses needed help. He had God's favor, but he needed others to help him serve the people. Moses went to his father-in-law, Jethro, for advice and counsel. Jethro told Moses how to delegate the authority to the twelve tribes of Israel. Moses got help and received it with gratitude. He was relieved of his problem. He did what God had called him to do for His people.

Pastors are called and chosen by God, but they can get overloaded with responsibilities. Pastors need those who are spiritually empowered by God to help implement and complete the work. Truly, there are saints working in some of the ministries without the Holy Spirit. This will lead to a spiritual breakdown in the flock. On the other hand, those who are not operating in the power of God need to get filled with the Holy Ghost. The power of the Holy Spirit is needed in all ministries. Those who are led by the spirit of God are the "sons of God" (Romans 8:14).

There are those who are trying to lead a holy ministry from God with unholy people. These people must get cleaned up before they can lead. The Word will surely clean His people every day. "Now ye are clean through the word which I have spoken unto you" (John 15:3). The Word and the Holy Spirit have to be in the saints for them to be ready to handle God's business. They must be saved, filled with the Holy Ghost, and delivered before taking on a ministry-leadership role.

The pastors after God's own heart are real; they are not wicked and vindictive. They are individuals with a view from heaven, promises, and provisions from God. Likewise, they are sold out for Jesus and depend on Jesus as their source. They cannot be bought because they will not compromise. Jesus gives them His divine favor, and it is fair. When Jesus gives you His favor, it is fair. He will give His favor to those whom He can trust. Can Jesus trust you to handle His favor?

Jesus has given His pastors divine favor. Pastors, when your bills are due, church members are out of order, you are misunderstood at home, and your days are tough, will Jesus trust you to wait on Him? You have to trust Jesus for everything. I have encountered these conditions, and they are very uncomfortable. I learned how to trust Jesus for everything. He has the divine orders and gives the orders to us. Moses found this to be true: he had to depend on God's orders. Moses was a pastor after God's own heart, and he was given God's divine favor.

We have pastors after God's own heart, and they have His favor on their lives. Some pastors have favor with God and with man. Today, I salute all pastors in the world who are standing for Jesus without compromise. It is good, men and women of God, when you are in His perfect will. I decree the divine favor of Jesus upon His pastors and that they are walking in His perfect will.

Moses was appointed by God; God is appointing pastors today for the end-time harvest. The earth is groaning for the manifestations of God (Romans 8:22). When Moses was a baby, his mother placed him in a little basket and put it in the river. The pharaoh's daughter found Moses. He was saved by the pharaoh's daughter for the purposes and plans of God.

"For promotion cometh neither from the east, nor from the west, nor from the south" (Psalm 75:6). The divine favor of God will give you a promotion. Furthermore, here is a testimony of the favor of God in my life. The divine favor has been on my family for many years, and I count it all joy. The Lord Jesus called me into youth ministry at an early age. The favor and the calling of Jesus for preaching were upon me, but I did not answer the call to preach until I was thirty years old. In those days, I continued to speak for youth-day events, women's days, and community events. I was excited, elated, and enjoyed being used by Jesus. However, it was in August 1984 when Jesus called me and qualified me to preach His gospel. It was on a Sunday, in the evening, after I had delivered the youth-day message at Good Hope Missionary Baptist Church, Wetumpka, Alabama.

That evening, when I returned home, the Holy Spirit overpowered me. I had to say, "Yes, Lord, I will obey and will preach Your Word." Moreover, each day for the next week, I would go to the same place in my bedroom to pray. Truly, the exact thing would happen. I talked to my pastor, late Rev. Dan Johnson; I talked to my brother, pastor, Dr. Claude A. Shuford, family members, and late Rev. Nelson Henry; I was told to stop running and answer the call to preach. It was a hard decision to make because our church did not believe in women preachers. Rev. Louise Hall told me if they allowed me to preach outside of the church, in front of the doors, to preach the Word. If I was not allowed to preach in the pulpit, just to preach where it was permitted. She said, "Just obey God and Jesus and preach wherever they allow you to preach."

I answered the call to preach, and I preached my initial sermon on September 30, 1984, at Good Hope Missionary Baptist Church in Wetumpka, Alabama, entitled I Cried, "Mercy." The church was full of people; some of the people had to stand. I was nervous at the beginning, but the Holy Spirit fell powerfully onto the church that night. Glory, hallelujah, to Jesus!

The favor of God allowed me to become the first Black female preacher to be licensed and ordained in the region during the National Baptist Convention, USA. "To God be the glory for the things He has done" (Lou Fellingham, "To God be the Glory"). People from all surrounding counties came to the initial sermon; some of them were shocked; some were shouting; some were spectators, and some were genuinely sincere. Some of the people wanted to see if the pastor was going to back down and not allow me to preach. They wanted to see if he allowed it to happen, what would be the consequences?

God's favor is awesome! God allowed the pastor and me to be used by Him in a mighty way. Therefore, today my husband and I have licensed, ordained, mentored, and pastored over fifty-five preachers or more in our church and Bible college: some of the women, including my biological daughter, Pastor Colenthia De'Von Milner-Wright, and some of my nieces. One of our nieces, Pastor Michele Milner-Copeland, is assigned as pastor at Global Word Fellowship, and our daughter is the senior pastor; they are doing an excellent job.

When I was called to preach, my pastor allowed me to preach from the floor; women were not allowed to go into the pulpit. Today, praise Jesus, in our ministry and in so many others around the world, women are allowed to preach in the pulpit. Today female preachers preach from the pulpit and pastor churches. God heard our cries and has brought deliverance to so many preachers. The favor that God and my father in the ministry, late Rev. Dan Johnson, granted to me will always be remembered and appreciated.

God's favor and His grace are sufficient for us, and He is an on-time God. Our good friend, Dottie Peoples, says, "He may not come when you want Him, but He is always right on time." He's an on-time God, yes! Jesus is always on time, sufficient, and a protector of His sheep.

The ministries that God called me to serve in have been great and rewarding to His people and me. He gave me three good pastors to work under and my younger brother, pastor, Dr. Claude A. Shuford. He purchased my first set of ministry books.

God allowed me to serve as a pastor, youth minister, assistant pastor, and twice as an interim pastor at the same church. I also served for fifteen years as a district missionary. God chose me as the pastor of the Good Hope Missionary Baptist Church, Wetumpka, Alabama. Our Jesus has given me twenty-seven years and nine months in ministry at one location. I am so thankful to Jesus for His favor.

"The LORD is [...] plenteous in mercy" (Psalm 103:8). "His mercy is everlasting; and his truth endureth to all generations" (Psalm 100:5). When I speak of the mercy and favor of Jesus, my eyes get filled with tears. He has been so good to me. The days of pain, suffering, and walking by faith have made me trust Jesus even more. I think about Job's and Joseph's experiences. They endured hardship as good soldiers, but God brought them out. He is my source of joy. The joy of the Lord is our strength (Nehemiah 8:10).

The years of ministry in my hometown have not been

easy. There were times that I was ridiculed, rejected, and not remembered, but Jesus was faithful. The Bible tells us that "a prophet is not without honour, but in his own country" (Mark 6:4). The Lord has carried me away from the red clay hills of Alabama. I have been to the nation's capital and abroad. His favor was upon my mother and dad. Mom was a great teacher of the Word, preacher, prayer warrior, supermom, loving grandmother, and worshipper. She was a loving wife to our dad, the late Robert Lee Shuford. My dad could pray and sing those old songs. He taught me a lot of good things. I really miss my mom and dad since they have gone to be with the Lord. The favor that their lives had was transferred to their children. The Lord has done great things for me, so I am glad (Psalm 126:3). His divine favor is upon the Shuford family, and we don't take it lightly. The Bible says when Job prayed for his friends, the captivity of Job changed. Our family has learned how to pray for those who despitefully misuse us and bless those who curse us (Romans 12:14).

Moreover, when saints do things God's way, He will turn things around. Our mom taught us to serve, love, and always respect the men and women of God. This teaching has been a blessing to us, her children, and her grandchildren.

In like manner, when people disrespect those who have

authority over them, they are headed for failure. It's only a manner of time for God to bring His wrath on rebellious people. Each day, we strive to keep our lives real and obey God. Thank you, God, Mom, and Dad, for your love and guidance!

The pastors the Lord allowed me to serve were very good mentors to my family and me. Likewise, their wives and their families were good to us. It was a pleasure and a great privilege to have served them. Today, I believe God gave me His favor because I respected my parents, pastors, leaders, and teachers. Give honor to whom honor is due (Romans 13:7). Therefore, in order for pastors to excel in the kingdom, they must be kingdom minded and have the spirit of obedience.

The kingdom mind is a transformed mind: "Be ye transformed by the renewing of your mind" (Romans 12:2). The Lord gave me a transformed mind. He renews my mind daily for His kingdom work. "Let this mind be in you, which was also in Christ Jesus" (Philippians 2:5). His grace was sufficient for me all the time, and He favored me. The days of my pastoring the church and leading God's people were challenging and rewarding. I will not change the destiny that God set for me because He made me a better person and a better preacher. "To God be the glory for the things He has done" (Lou Fellingham,

"To God be the Glory").

The divine favor of Jesus is upon my life, and He has anointed me to preach the gospel. I want my life to be pleasing to Jesus every day! I thank God for His divine favor, goodness, and mercy. The poem below will give a message of God's favor:

"God's Favor"

> He gave me His divine favor.
>
> Jesus is powerful and able.
>
> Jesus showed me a better way.
>
> His plans carried me day by day.
>
> The Lord's favor is fair.
>
> He is everywhere!
>
> The just, the kind, and the true,
>
> Jesus's love will carry you through.
>
> The wind may sometimes blow.
>
> God will carry you forevermore.
>
> The just shall live by faith.
>
> He shall give an eternal home to stay.
>
> His divine favor is like the choicest gold.
>
> Jesus is as sweet as the honeycomb.
>
> I found out without a doubt

Jesus's favor and love will bring you out.

Golden Nuggets by the Late Bishop Frank T. Bozeman

- Fair-weather days in life help prepare you for stormy days.
- You have the faith to weather your storms; go ahead and shout, "Victory!"
- Move to the beat of the Holy Spirit.
- Where He leads me, I will follow; I will go with Him all the way.
- All is good: praise your way out of the pain.
- I cannot help myself; praise is what I do.
- Storms come, and they go, but I still let my praise flow.
- Praise is not an option; it is a mandate.
- Press your way through the pain.
- Have a thank-you fit.
- I am more than a conqueror.
- We speak showers of blessings and overflow of joy in the lives of our family and friends.
- You are blessed in the city in the fields, going out and coming in.
- Make up your mind to serve Jesus every day.
- We have a mind to live for Jesus all of our days.
- If it had not been for Jesus on our sides, we would

not be here.

- You got your lesson.
- Jesus died on the cross for all our sins; thank you, Jesus.
- Run to do His will.
- Get ready for your breakthrough blessings.
- It is a supernatural turnaround: *shondo*!
- A word of power: you are not alone. The Bible says, "Lo, I am with you always, even unto the end of the world" (Matthew 28:20).
- When we think of the goodness of Jesus and all He has done for us, our souls shout, "Hallelujah, thank You, God, for saving us!"
- Thank You, Jesus, for all Your benefits. Jesus is loading you with His benefits daily.
- Need directions? Seek and trust God. He will lead and guide you.
- Oh, how excellent it is when we show love and forgive others.
- When others treat you wrong, love them with God's love.
- Try Jesus: He is wonderful.
- Love covers a multitude of sins.
- Whatever is holding you back or down, drop it and let it go!

- Let Jesus pick you up and watch Him turn things around for you.
- Jesus is awesome, and His grace is amazing.
- God bless you!
- Jesus gives us new mercies every day.
- He carries us from strength to strength and from glory to glory.
- "But my God shall supply all your need according to his riches in glory by Christ Jesus" (Philippians 4:19).
- Do you need a word from the Lord? He said that He loads us with benefits every day.
- I had to learn how to wait on Jesus; it is very important for all leaders to wait on Jesus. Do you have the patience to wait?

The Bible says, "But they that wait upon the Lord shall renew their strength, they shall mount up with wings as eagles, they shall run, and not be weary, and they shall walk, and not faint" (Isaiah 40:31). On Sundays and every day, we must have a real passion for Jesus Christ; He is our Lord and our Savior.

You are one step away from your breakthrough: don't let go of your miracle; move forward with Jesus guiding you. I pray that Jesus will paralyze your pain, release your pressures, and press you toward your promises. Be not dismayed about whatever you are going through: God will take care of you.

Our thanks are to all of you for the showers of love and support. May the blessings of the Lord overtake you!

I thank You, Jesus, for my birthday on Resurrection Sunday in 2013. Thank You, Jesus: You have done great things for us.

He saved us, changed our lives, and made us whole. He has done so much for us that we cannot tell it all. We remember when Jesus saved us; do you remember when He saved you? I got filled with the Holy Ghost in Rome, Georgia, in 1985—that was awesome, and I will never forget that experience. Today, I am moving in the power of the Holy Ghost, walking in the right directions, walking with Jesus, waiting on Jesus, worshipping with Jesus, and proclaiming His Word. God has got this process, and I am glad about it. He told me not to worry and to let Jesus fight my battles. Oh, yes, I am divinely connected to Jesus, and I am a "joint-heir" (Romans 8:17). In like manner, I am divinely favored by God. C. S. Lewis said, "Though our feelings come and go, His love for us does not."[2] Therefore, saints, you are loved and divinely favored by God. Your life speaks volumes to others. You are a living testimony and an example to others.

Let your light shine so men can see your good works

and glorify the Father in heaven. He has given you His favor, and His mercy is everlasting. Great is His faithfulness, morning by morning, new mercies we see (Thomas Chisholm, "Great Is Thy Faithfulness").

Pastors, leaders in the government and in every area of life need the favor of Jesus resting upon them. Some people don't have favor and want it, and others have it and don't appreciate it. We can't take God's favor for granted and can't get the credit for having God's favor in our lives. However, the favor of Jesus is upon our lives, and we thank Him for His favor, grace, and mercy.

The picture below shows the smiles on our faces, and they are real. We were truly thankful. God's favor was increasing upon us with each year we had in the ministry, and He kept us humble. We are grateful for having favor with God and favor with man.

May Jesus continue to bless all of His children with His richest blessings and His favor! We, Bishops Frank T. and Hurdis Bozeman, always say that it's God's favor upon us. Therefore, we can't take any credit for what Jesus has done in our lives. Jesus has done so much for us that we can't begin to tell about all of His goodness. Proverbs 10:22 says, "The blessing of the LORD, it maketh rich, and he addeth no sorrow to it."

Hallelujah, Jesus! Thank You for Your blessings and Your favor. I will forever praise and worship You. You are my source of joy, power, and strength.

CHAPTER 3

Wolves in the Sheepfold

Pastors and leaders have to deal with so many people with all types of personalities and objectives. There are some with a sabotage spirit, a backstabbing spirit, and a sarcastic spirit. There are so many unfair people with the spirit of a wolf in our churches, schools, communities, workplaces, and many other areas. The wolf spirit comes from the thief, the enemy. The thief is the devil. The Bible gives a very clear view of the thief; in John 10:10, it reads: "The thief cometh not, but for to steal, and to kill, and to destroy: I am come that they might have life, and that they might have it more abundantly." In this text, Jesus was saying that the thief is the devil.

The devil is coming to steal, kill, and destroy the sheep. Who are the sheep? You are the sheep (the saints), and there are wolves in the sheepfold. Therefore, the scripture says that Jesus came to give more abundant life to us. The abundant life includes Jesus's protection: Jesus will protect His sheep from the wolves. The thief is the enemy, and he works hard to destroy the sheep. The enemy's job is to devour, mislead, displace, destroy, depress, deplete, and kill the sheep. In a spiritual battle, the sheep's spirit can get wounded or killed by the thief.

A wounded sheep (saint) has to be cared for properly. You can't treat a wound with unclean hands. The Bible says in Psalm 24 that we must have clean hands and a clean heart. Some sheep (saints) are being treated by those with unclean hands, and the dirt rubs off into the wound. The sheep are in more danger when the thief is in the camp and when those who are working for the Great Shepherd are unclean. This is double trouble, dangerous and disastrous for the sheep. The Shepherd of the sheep, according to the Bible in John 10:2–4, says:

> But he that entereth by the door is the Shepherd of the sheep. To him the porter openeth; and the sheep hear his voice and he calleth His own sheep by name, and leadeth them out. And when […] he goeth before them and the sheep follow him; for they know his voice.

In like manner, the sheep are those who hear the voice of Jesus and follow Him. The wolf is the devil, and he wants to devour the sheep. The Word of God says,

> But he that is a hireling, and not the Shepherd, whose own the sheep are not, seeth the

wolf coming, and leaveth the sheep, and fleeth and the wolf catcheth them, and scattereth the sheep. The hireling fleeth, because he is a hireling, and careth not for the sheep.

John 10:12–13

The person in the household of faith who is a hireling is the one working for the devil. They are not workers for Jesus. Therefore, in the body of Christ, we have wolves in sheep's clothing; they are not of the sheepfold. In John 10:16, the Bible tells us, "And other sheep I have, which are not of this fold: them also I must bring, and they shall hear my voice; and there shall be one fold, and one shepherd."

Again, the wolf is the devil, and he is the enemy of the sheep. The book of Isaiah gives us a clear view; it reads in Isaiah 53:6, "All we like sheep have gone astray; we have turned every one to his own way and the Lord hath laid on him the iniquity of us all."

The sheep, God's children, have salvation through Jesus Christ. When the wolf comes into the sheepfold, it is important for the undershepherd to protect the sheep. There are some in the fold who have not met Christ, and the saints cannot allow the wolves to destroy them. Also, those in the fold who are saved have to be protected. Thank

God for the blood of Jesus: it covers us and protects us. The blood of Jesus will never lose its power.

The children of Jesus Christ are called "sheep," and the wolves are called the "devil," "enemy," "demons," and "adversary." In the sheepfold, there are several types of sheep. The undershepherd (pastor) has to know them and protect them. In many modern-day churches, there are several ministers to help the pastor. However, there are some in sheep clothing who have a wolf spirit. In the world, there are about 1,000 different types of sheep. Moreover, every sheep looks different, and sometimes, a shepherd cannot tell them apart. Yet, sheep can tell each other apart. This is good and is extra good in the body of Christ because saints know each other.

The Bible talks about sheep more than any other animals; sheep are mentioned more than 400 times. The children of God have a lot in common with sheep. Sheep are followers, and we are followers of Christ. In Matthew 25:32–33, the Bible says;

> And before him shall be gathered all nations: and he shall separate them one from another, as a shepherd divideth his sheep from the goats: And he shall set the sheep on his right hand, but the goats on the left.

This means that Jesus is coming back and that He will gather His sheep. He will do the separating procedure on that great separation day. Jesus will place the sheep (His children) on the right side and the goats (the devil's children) on the left side. Those who are on the left side are the unholy, the unrighteous, the unsaved, and the unjust. Those who are on Jesus's right side are the holy, the righteous, the saved, and the just. We all must be ready for the coming of the Lord: the wolf has to be abolished. Therefore, there is a mandate for saints to help win souls for Christ. We can't allow the wolf to take the sheep out. The wolves are in the sheepfold, but God will help the saints identify them. The saints must have a strong spirit of discernment. In the sheepfold, there are those dressed up like sheep, but they are wolves.

Saints, open your eyes. You must ask Jesus to empower you to see the evil spirits. The wolves are sent by the devil to kill, steal, and destroy. The wolves come to the sheep, disguised as good sheep. A wolf's heart is vicious; they are false prophets who come to the sheepfold in sheep clothing, but inward, they are wolves.

Wolves are discerned by their fancy talk: they speak of supernatural things, but they are ravening wolves with murderous hearts. Their appetite is voracious. In Matthew 7:15, the Bible says, "Beware of false prophets, which come to you in sheep's clothing, but inwardly they are like ravening wolves." The wolves are dressed up on the outside, and on the inside, they are messed up. The wolves come to take over, destroy, and mislead the sheep. They will divide the God-given vision. Sometimes, wolves will make a mockery of the servant of God and the ministry if they are not rebuked and chastised. We shall know the wolf by their fruit (Matthew 7:16).

So, when the pastor has been given a *vision* from God for His people, the wolves will want to stop his or her vision. The wolves are in the sheepfold. There are some individuals in the church who dress up well externally, but they are not fixed internally. They will take over and produce a spirit of *division*. Some have motives and schemes that are unholy and unrighteous.

How do pastors handle the wolves? God has given us a formula in His Word. He told pastors to "reprove, rebuke, exhort with all longsuffering and doctrine" (2 Timothy 4:2). Today, more than I have seen, Jesus is uncovering, exposing, and getting the wolves out of the sheepfold. Wolves are in the sheepfold; believe me: it's the truth.

When was the last time you identified a person in ministry who had a wolf spirit? They are more visible and bold in ministry today than they were ten years ago. The pastor has to identify the wolf and call the spirit out by the power of the Holy Ghost. These spirits have to become null and void in ministry in the mighty name of Jesus. Saints and prayer warriors must be empowered by the Holy Ghost to cast out demons. "The kingdom suffereth violence, and the violent take it by force" (Matthew 11:12). Pastors cannot stand by and allow the wolves to destroy innocent and uncovered sheep. They must take a stand in the power of the Holy Ghost. The sheep will go astray, this is their nature, but the undershepherd must bring them back into the fold. Saints must be intercessors and must intercede with the undershepherd for the sheep. The sheep may wander away from the sheepfold, but they will hear and know the voice of the shepherd. The sheep who will not hear the shepherd's voice are those who are rebellious or do not belong to the sheepfold. The sheep who belong to the sheepfold (the ministry) will not take heed to the voice of a stranger. The Bible tells us, "And a stranger will they not follow, but will flee from him: for they know not the voice of strangers" (John 10:5).

Yes, there are workers in ministry who are wolves. Wolves are in the sheepfold, but the power of the Holy Ghost will draw them to Christ or will drive them away. We have the *authority* in the Word of God to speak deliverance. We have the *assurance* to believe that His Word shall come to pass. Also, we have the *availability* of His promises. The wolves in the sheepfold shall be *abolished* by Jesus.

"Jesus"

Jesus, Jesus, He will provide.

Jesus, Jesus, the Lord by our sides.

Jesus, Jesus, you can trust Him as your guide.

Jesus, Jesus, in Him you can reside.

Just a whisper and a sweet, gentle breeze:

I heard Him when I was down on my knees.

Without a shadow of a doubt,

Jesus will surely bring you out.

When your heart is sinking kind of low,

Look to Jesus: He will show you where to go.

He always knows; just trust Him at His word.

He still feeds the little birds.

Jesus told me to look and live.

To His children, He freely gives.

Day by day, He sends the latter rain.

His healing wings erase all pain.

Jesus will help pastors identify and abolish

the wolves in the sheepfold. Consequently, all pastors, leaders, and laity have a plight in life, and they must trust Jesus to accomplish the victory. The Lord Jesus gave me this poem concerning the saints' plight:

"The Saints' Plight"

> You sat and watched my pain.
> Without any presentation, they put me to shame.
> Some people play dreadful and destructive games.
> Without a doubt, they tried to destroy my name.
> You can't tell a lot of people anything when they
> are wrong.
> They are so hyped up and have a mind of their
> own.
> The time will come when people wish they had
> spiritual ears to hear.
> They will call on Jesus mightily, and He will not
> be near.
> The Holy Bible they better read and take heed.
> One day they will reap all of their good and bad
> deeds.

When you keep the faith and never lose hope,

The spiritual hymns of praise will be on the right
note.

It's already done, and we can truly see.

Jesus, saints, will soon be set free.

During the pandemic, I experienced some of the most difficult days in my life. I watched my husband go through trials and tribulations for two years. He stayed in the hospital and rehab at different times for over 180 days. He did not lose his faith, and he fought the kidney disease until Jesus said, "Well done!" The nurses were jewels, and God gave me two poems concerning His servants.

"Heavenly Duties"

I wonder how they are working up in heaven.

Some of the first responders work from seven to
seven.

The nurses and healthcare workers work from
dawn to dusk,

Comforting and taking care of us.

They are very busy administering meds from a big
computer tray.

The wheels are turning fast as the nurse rolls

    swiftly away.

Their noise is heard at times down the hall.

A few precious items sometimes begin to fall.

I don't try to understand the Master's great plan.

Every chance that I get, I try to give the nurses a

    helping hand.

The first responders down here need all of us

To stand up and give them a big cheer.

There are no tears in heaven and no deaths.

On the earth, the poor die and those with great

    wealth.

Some of the heavenly-assigned duties on the earth

    often go unnoticed,

But their labor is recorded in heaven and reported.

"Nurses Are Jewels"

Nurses are jewels; they work overtime.

They give you that extra push so you can survive.

Some sacrifice their life for the call of duty.

We must give them their due diligence and

appreciate their beauty.

Oh, yes, don't forget the days of working in this
horrible pandemic.

It has overloaded our nurses, and their tasks are
too many.

There are big tasks at home, at work, and in other
places.

They have numerous tasks, duties,

And their desks are filled with so many cases.

I wonder what we would do if nurses did not work
on me and you.

They truly help to carry us through.

The shifts change, the nagging, the very sick, and
the crying patients.

Wow, all of this stuff makes nurses leave their
stations.

Doctors, patients, and families fuss and call their
names.

It makes the nurses pray harder to embrace the
change.

How long will the headaches from this ugly
pandemic last?

The nurses are tired, Lord Jesus: they need a
   break fast.

Hurdis

Your cry has been deeply expressed and heard.

The pain and agony that you feel are erased with
   God's Word.

Calm your spirit down, and don't fret.

Jesus Christ has never failed any of His children yet.

Don't get caught up in the cares and pressures of life.

Remember, Hurdis: your main focus must be on
   Christ.

Some of the days ahead will be cloudy and a little
   blue.

You just keep on looking to Jesus; He will see you
   through.

The wisdom, the knowledge, and the understanding
   of your tasks

Will help preserve you, shape you, and give you
   peace that will forever last.

It's personal to you, but you can't get stuck or off
   track.

The good Lord Jesus has given you a strong back.

When will you know that it's Him and not the

enemy all the time?

My dear Hurdis, you are going through this

journey just fine.

Listen to the birds sing and the whisper of the

wind breeze.

Put things that you are doing on pause; will you

stop, for a moment, please!

Get up, wash your tears away, stand up strong on

this beautiful day.

You are on the mark and ready to immediately be

gone on your merry way.

When I think of the goodness of Jesus and all that He has done for me, my soul shouts, "Hallelujah! Thank You, Jesus, for saving me." There may be mountains that we have to speak to and valleys that we have to endure, but when Jesus gets involved, He takes care of everything.

CHAPTER 4

Pastors Pray Your Way Through

What *is* prayer?

Prayer is our communication with God; it is a dialogue, not a monologue. I have prayed on my knees, on the floor with my face down, in the shower, in my car, sitting in the midst of people on the bus, on the airplane, and in many other places. Prayer is necessary, and prayer works. Moreover, I am a praying woman of God, and I truly believe in the power of prayer. The dictionary says that "prayer" is "a solemn request for help or expression of thanks addressed to God or an object of worship."[3] I prefer the first definition given above: "Prayer is our communication with God."

What does "prayer" mean to you? There are different types of prayers; pastors have prayed all of them during their pastoral assignment. How did pastors make it through difficult times, vicissitudes of life, trials, tribulations, comebacks, tears, pain, burdens, joblessness, confusion, economic disadvantages, disappointments, the good times as well as the bad times?

It was the power of prayer and fasting that gave me

a miraculous breakthrough. Prayer works. Moreover, pastors, you can call on Jesus for divine help. Jesus left pastors, leaders, and His children a Comforter. Yes, Jesus left His children the Holy Spirit. The Holy Spirit is groaning and making intersessions that we cannot speak. The Holy Spirit is needed in our prayer life every day. In the earthly realm, someone is praying for you right now. Don't lose hope, don't give up, don't throw in the towel, and don't beat up on yourself. It's going to get better; trust Jesus.

On the global prayer call, we are decreeing a twenty-four-hour miraculous turnaround. Prayers are going forth for pastors and their families. Saints, prayer works. Oh yes, saints are interceding for pastors because some of the pastors are in their comfort zone. They are afraid to launch out into the deep.

When God spoke to me years ago concerning my next kingdom assignment, I did not move forward. I was reluctant to launch out into the deeper things of God. There were prayer warriors fasting and praying for me daily. Moreover, when God gave me the next assignment, I should have fasted, prayed, and moved immediately. However, I listened to the people's requests, and I remained in God's permissive will.

We are praying for spiritual leaders to move in God's perfect will. I am saying Jesus will forgive you when you are disobedient, but you have to face the consequences. Also, people have to forgive pastors for being disobedient, and pastors have to forgive people. Yes, pastors fall short of the glory of God, and they must ask God for His forgiveness. Oh yes, move out of the way and let God correct His pastors. We must fast, pray, obey God, and trust Him to correct His leaders. He will lead you into all truth when you trust Him.

Saints, in so many cases, run ahead of God, and things get out of spiritual alignment. I have compassion for pastors who are crying out for help because there were days that I had to cry out to God for help. I can identify with some of their problems. However, some of the people in God's house treat their pastors as if they were not human.

Don't expect the pastor to get everything right. Pastors need God's love and need the saints to love them unconditionally. Some pastors are praying and walking in God's perfect will. Jesus loves pastors who have forgiven the saints, and the saints must forgive them. Pastors continue to pray, obey God's voice, and move forward with His plans for their lives. Remember Jeremiah 29:11 (NKJV): "For I know the thoughts that I think toward you, says the LORD, thoughts of peace and not of evil, to give you a future and a hope."

You are destined to fulfill His kingdom assignment

for your life. The children of Israel asked God for a king because they were tired of the judges. God granted them their request and gave them King Saul. Saul's name means "asked of God." Moreover, when God gave Israel King Saul, He gave him to them with conditions attached. In 1 Samuel 12:14–15 (ESV), the Bible says,

> If you will fear the LORD and serve him and obey his voice and not rebel against the commandment of the LORD, and if both you and the king who reigns over you will follow the LORD your God, it will be well. But if you will not obey the voice of the LORD, but rebel against the commandment of the LORD, then the hand of the LORD will be against you and your king.

In like manner, when God gives a church a pastor after God's own heart, He will lead them. The pastor and the people must be in unity, pray constantly, study the Word of God, and obey God's instructions. Jesus will give the time for the pastor to enter the ministry, and He will give the departure time. Yes, Jesus knows when it is time for a pastor to move and knows when it's not time.

Pastors must have a strong prayer life. Likewise, if they are married, they need a strong praying spouse.

The pastor's assignment is given by Jesus. It must be

embarked upon when Jesus has given the release and the anointing. Jesus knows when it's time to give the promotion to preachers and their divine provisions. Oh yes, saints, Jesus knows when it is time to send a pastor into transition and change. He also knows when it's time to place the feet of the pastor on new territory.

Trust me: I am a living witness; Jesus will put you in the right place and at the right time—with the right people. The pastor must know that when God says no, He means no. In the book of Samuel, God gave the people of Israel specific directives to follow. He gives pastors directives to follow all through the day and at the appointed time. Therefore, if they do not follow God's directives, they will be in serious trouble with God. I believe God is giving pastors, leaders, laity, and others directives to follow today that will help bring in an end-time harvest.

Pastors keep on getting it right and refuse to get it wrong: obey Jesus, not man. Pastors, will you continue to obey Jesus's voice and move under the guidance of the Holy Spirit? He is saying to you, "It is time for you to pray My Word and stand on My Word." You cannot compromise! The Word of God will not change.

God is the same yesterday, today, and forever (Hebrews 13:8). Speak Jesus's Word, praise Jesus's Word, preach Jesus's Word, teach Jesus's Word, and by all means, live Jesus's Word. Jesus is waiting on you to obey His Word all the time. Jesus is waiting on you to finish your kingdom assignment with His authority and assurance. If you have changed positions, places, or plans, you must move by His spirit.

He is not slack concerning His promises to you (2 Peter 3:9). Pastors, when it's time to launch out into the deep, you must go with gladness and obedience. Jesus sees your tears; Jesus knows your fears and your pain.

Trust Jesus for the process, pray, and go with Him all the way. Jesus gave me a new song during my transitional time as a pastor. This new song is a blessing. Jesus took the pain and hurt away when He gave me songs, sermons, and poems. He has heard the cry of pastors. He hears how you, as a believer, cry. Jesus will answer your cry. He will heal you and set you free.

Jesus told me during my transition to say to a wonderful young minister these words: "Don't worry about how He will bless you; stay committed to the plans and the purposes of Jesus." These words were for me, and they meant: "Don't worry about Jesus taking care of things; you just stay committed to Jesus." He takes care of all things. Therefore, if a believer is going through tribulations, they need a word from the Lord. The Bible has all the answers.

The Bible says He will not do anything until He reveals it to His servants, the prophets (Amos 3:7). At this time, the office of the prophet is needed every day. Pastors need to have someone to speak into their lives. Jesus hears the prayers and cries of His pastors and sends them real prophets. "The righteous cry, and the LORD heareth, and He delivereth them out of all of their troubles" (Psalm 34:17).

"The Water Was Troubled"

The water was troubled; I rushed into a panic.

My heart was pounding, and I said, "I can't stand it!"

The days were long, cloudy, and blue.

My faith was assured with hope, and they both saw me through!

The voice of God was not heard.

So I looked around, and I was disturbed.

I cried as the strong winds sounded loud.

My God, my God, I did not stand proud!

There was a silent fear.

I was afraid that my God was not near.

I could not hold my peace.

But out of the darkness, Jesus gave me sweet relief!

Jesus said, "My child, you are not alone.

Stand up tall, look at me, and be strong."

Now I see that You were always there for me.

I must move forward with haste and go where You
want me to be!

Jesus gave me joy, unspeakable and full of glory.

He gave me true worship and added to my life
story.

Jesus said to me, "My child, you are finally free.

Your cries and your pain have come up unto Me!"

The waters covered you, but you did not drown.

Your sufferings and frustrations did not show a
big frown.

The anger, the hurt, and the fear—Jesus caused
them to disappear.

Your blessings are coming forth before the end of
this year.

Our Lord, Jesus, has given us, pastors, so many wom-
en and men to work with. We thank Him for entrusting
His children to us. Bishop and I thank Jesus for our bi-

ological and spiritual daughter, Senior Pastor Colenthia Milner-Wright, our niece, Pastor Michele Milner-Copeland, our friends, late Bishop, Dr. Sherri Solomon-Davis, and late Deacon Jimmy Davis, also Apostle Jimmie and Apostle Kathy Taylor, Evangelist Rochelle Alston and Mr. James Alston, Pastor Teresa Solomon, Pastor Tammy Hudgons, Minister Allyn Solomon, Rev. Craig Milner, Sister Twanna Brown, Minister Felecia McBride, Minister Billie Taylor, Rev. Laura Cain, Minister Chaundra Orsborne, Sister Dorothy Leonard, Sister Angela Vines, Prophetess Ruby Grays, Minister Sheryl Austin, Bishop Dave Greathouse, Bishop Kenneth Lewis, Pastor Kimberly Lewis, and a host of spiritual sons and daughters. Some of them have supported our ministry and been our prayer warriors for many years.

Furthermore, if you have been old or young and going through transition, you can testify that you need others to pray, assist, and support you.

Thank You, Jesus! You are everywhere, all-seeing and all-powerful. Jesus takes care of all our needs "according to His riches in glory by Christ Jesus" (Philippians 4:19).

When we go through as saints, we must remember that we are a product of Jesus. He made man in His own image. We shall not allow anything to separate us from the love of Christ Jesus; His love will carry us all the way. Hallelujah!

Pastors and saints, when you obey God, you shall walk forward in abundance, favor, joy, peace, faith, and your Jesus-given kingdom assignment. In closing: it's time to see the manifestation of God's Word carry pastors to another place, dimension, position, job, assignment, appointment, and realm in Jesus! Pastors must pray and always obey the voice of Jesus. They keep on praying with assurance, confidence, wisdom, and the Word and pray in the spirit. Prayer works!

Original picture by Bishop Hurdis Shuford-Bozeman

CHAPTER 5

The Spirit of Betrayal

The betrayal spirit is a dangerous one, and it is destructive. This spirit produces deception, death, lies, betrayal, and destruction. Moreover, this spirit carries the spirit of assassination. In the body of Christ and in the secular arena, there are those who will assault, assassinate, annihilate, and obliterate your character. In like manner, they will try to kill your vision, wipe out your ministry, campaign, victory, company, and resources. Therefore, this spirit is a very dangerous, deceptive, and cunning one; it is prevalent in our country today more than ever. We have seen, in this millennium, the snake biting and the python sucking the life out of people's spirits.

The word "betrayal" means to "deceive," "misguide," or "corrupt." It can also mean to "deliver" or "reveal the enemy by treachery," "be disloyal," "break a presumptive contract," "trust," and "confidence."

When we look at our nation today, we see the worst scenario playing out right before our eyes. Our pastors and leaders in the political community need to have a very strong spirit of discernment and divine guidance from the Lord of lords.

In Matthew 26:47–48 (NIV), the Bible says that Judas betrayed Jesus Christ:

> While He was still speaking, Judas, one of the twelve, arrived. With him was a large crowd armed with swords and clubs, sent from the chief priests and the elders of the people. Now the betrayer had arranged a signal with them: "The one I kiss is the man; arrest him."

After Judas betrayed Jesus, he returned the thirty pieces of silver that he had been paid to do that. Judas said, "I have sinned by betraying innocent blood." But they said to Judas, "What's that to us? See to it" (Matthew 27:4, NKJV). The spirit of betrayal, which was controlling Judas, led him to his death.

Sometimes, things seem right to people but are contradictory to the Word of God. People will lead you to death if you don't discern their wicked betrayal spirit. The Bible tells us, "The wages of sin is death, but the gift of God is eternal life" (Romans 6:23). On the other hand, just as Judas betrayed Jesus, there are those in church, Congress, Senate, the White House, and statehouses in so many other places around the world operating in the spirit of betrayal.

Judas knew who Jesus was and was taught by Jesus, but he still betrayed Him. The good thing about the situation: Jesus knew who Judas was, and He saw the deceptive betrayal spirit. Do you see the snakes and tricky spirits that are in operation in the USA and other nations today? It is so awful, disgusting, and heartbreaking. Some of our pastors, political leaders, and others are engaged in the spirit of betrayal. They are forcing and encouraging others to participate in their spiritual wickedness.

When you encounter the spirit of betrayal among those in your circle, flee from it, denounce it, rebuke it, and ask the Holy Spirit to give you His guidance. In like manner, pastors and leaders need to discern the spirit of betrayal and various spirits that are in operation today so they can help themselves and others. Some of the sheep in church and the leaders in the nation will look like sheep, act like sheep, but they are goats. They refuse to hear the voice of Jesus; they are listening to strangers and are sold out to the enemy.

The spirit of discernment is one of the spirits that rested on Jesus; read Isaiah 11:2–3: it gives the seven spirits that rested upon Jesus. Everything that Jesus had, we should desire. The Bible says, "Let this mind be in you, which was also in Christ Jesus" (Philippians 2:5). Jesus had the spirit of discernment, wisdom, knowledge, counsel, might, the fear of the Lord, and understanding; all of these are valuable and vital for those in leadership.

Judas betrayed Jesus. Are you betraying someone in leadership or in laity? Some of you have walked with your leader in ministry, sat at their table and ate with them, rode in their car, spent their money, and been given spiritual guidance by them. But you are still backstabbing and betraying your leader. Lord Jesus, help us all!

Judas knew who Jesus was, and he walked with Him. Also, he was taught by Jesus. What is so awesome and interesting about the situation is that Jesus knew Judas was a betrayer.

The spirit of discernment is needed in the workplace, in church, at home, and in every area of your life. The gift of discernment is a must for ministries to operate effectively. The Lord Jesus gave me this prophetic word over five years ago: God is exposing these destructive spirits that are trying to infiltrate the righteous. Saints, the spirit of discernment must be very keen. Moreover, the python spirit comes to suck the life out of God's preachers and those who are righteous. The black-widow spirit is on the move; it comes to give a poisonous bite. The bite infiltrates control and releases misleading doctrines.

Saints, watch out for these cunning spirits that present ideas and their doctrines in a new way. These spirits are used to tear down good leadership, honorable character, and progressive ministries and weaken the mind of saints. The Judas spirit must be exposed! There are so many backbiting, backstabbing, and betrayal spirits in operation today. The spirit of betrayal was the one that Judas had when he betrayed Jesus. It is prevalent in this world today. However, we are not afraid; we must be watchful warriors pulling down strongholds! God said, "Satan, your kingdom shall come down" (Shirley Caesar, "Satan, We're Gonna Tear Your Kingdom Down").

The universal church has suffered enough lies, persecutions, backstabbing—all types of sins and egocentric views. God is watching all of us, and it's time for a spiritual checkup, spiritual ID checkup, and wake-up call.

Warning comes before destruction. Yes, Jesus is loving, just, forgiving, merciful, kind, saving, and everything that you need Him to be. Also, He is the only wise judge, our heavenly Father. He wants us to repent and turn completely to Him. Jesus loves us, but He hates sin. He died for you and for all of us, and He is married to the backslider. These spirits must be abolished, and the Holy Spirit must take control. Therefore, if you need to be saved, give your life to Jesus now and turn from your wicked ways. If you are saved and listening for instructions, tune in to the prophetic sound; it has a sound of release! Jesus is releasing repentance, restoration, renewal, righteousness, revival, rescue, realness, and much more. Put those holy hands up and say, "I surrender all; Jesus, I receive You as my personal Savior now."

My Personal Testimony

The Lord allowed me to be a loving, kind, and good pastor to my family, friends, church members, and others. The sheep whom God assigned to the pastor taught me as I was teaching them. "Teaching is an intellectual experience."[4] Moreover, God allowed me to serve in ministry for twenty-seven years in one location. I served, for eleven years and eight months, as the pastor and, for fifteen years and four months, as a youth-minister district missionary and assistant pastor. The Lord has His plans, His purposes for our lives. Therefore, I had to endure hardness like a good soldier.

The ministry is a good one, but there is always room for growth. The Lord Jesus would give me His instructions for His sheep, but some of the sheep would not receive His instructions. There were days I was in dismay and disappointed. But Jesus would send a word of encouragement through my husband, daughter, sisters, brothers, mom, pastors, and others. As pastors, we have to receive from others. Sometimes, He will send intercessors and ministers from other ministries to encourage you. Our Lord, Jesus, has revealed to me so many times the intent of the rebellious sheep. However, I must pray, love, and continue to be faithful. He has shown me the Jezebel spirit in some of His sheep, the Absalom spirit, the Judas spirit, and the spirit of error.

Also, Jesus has corrected me and put me back on track so I can handle the problems properly. I thank Jesus for the spirit of discernment. It has worked in my life so many times. It is still a mighty gift in my life. My sister, the late pastor Charlena Kay Miller, prayed for my spiritual eyes to open. She said, "The Lord is going to open your eyes, and your spirit of discernment will be even greater." When I went to church the next day, the spirits that I saw operate were a frightening experience. God showed me what I needed to be praying for and what I needed to openly and privately rebuke as a pastor. Since that day, I have grown to another dimension in this gift. Praise Jesus!

The Judas spirit was revealed to me in some of the sheep in a rare form. In September 2011, the Lord had told me that there was an attack coming my way. He said that some of the sheep would try to make a mockery of my ministry. The Lord showed the same thing to some of my prayer warriors and intercessors. The Judas spirit was very strong at that time, and my prayers had to be intensified. The Judas spirit started to produce lies and deliver a negative message to the church and community. Our God is awesome; He did not allow us to confront the sheep. He instructed us to fast, pray, love, and forgive. I cried, smiled, and held my head up because vengeance is the Lord's. Truly, saints, all I wanted to do was retire and move on as God had told me to do.

I deserved to get a monthly stipend, but it was not available to me. The truth has to be told because there are pastors without retirement, health insurance, and basic needs. I was blessed to have insurance and retirement pay from my job. Moreover, God wanted me to learn to trust Him for everything; God is my source. The Lord was calling me from the pastoral ministry. He told me that it was for a season. I was to preach, teach, and minister in church and in many places as a prophetess. He told me not to take the title of a prophetess, just operate in the office and use the gift. His voice brought a drastic change into my life and the life of the church. God told me to leave for three years, and I tried to stay until the building was paid off. I was in God's permissive will instead of being in His perfect will.

The third time God told me to move on, I was slain in the spirit. When Jesus allowed me to get up off of the floor, I quickly obeyed Him. Yes, He got my attention, and I was afraid. Some of the sheep were hurt, sad, confused, and some of the saints were angry. The more I poured out to them from my heart, the more I was rejected. Today, I am thankful because the event helped me push myself into my destiny. The rejection was good for me because if I had been received, I might have stayed. In like manner, among those who had forgiveness in their hearts against me, some of the people were happy for me to leave, and some were sad. Therefore, the Judas spirit brought about the spirit of error. This spirit of error hurt many of the sheep and produced a hostile church environment. The Judas spirit carries a spirit of assassination, corruption, treachery, and disloyalty.

I praise and thank Jesus for bringing healing, restoration, and change to the church. He blesses them mightily today. Saints, this is a cry of a pastor with experience and God-fearing humility. I want to help others, warn pastors and the sheep, and bring healing. I am not perfect, and He is still working on me daily. My walk with God is stronger, and I am going all the way with Jesus!

The days and nights were long when I had to move on. There was a time when I cried and prayed for hours, but God gave me His deliverance. I am awakening to a new day and a new season of transition and change. God is good. What the enemy meant for evil, God turned around for good (Genesis 50:20). It was good for the church and me.

Yes, change hurts and makes people angry, but God knows best. He brought all of us to a new order. The Lord had shifted the ministry and put in place His leadership. In like manner, it was time for me to move to the next assignment. My husband, Bishop Frank T. Bozeman, our daughter, Pastor Colenthia Milner-Wright, David Wright, my siblings, some of my friends, my grandchildren, my pastor, his wife, my moderator, some of the ministers, and a few of the members encouraged me daily. To God be the glory for the things He has done!

I had spent almost forty years in one church, ministering in various areas. God allowed me to serve as a member, youth minister, assistant pastor, interim pastor (twice), pastor, and in many areas of ministry. I am truly thankful for the blessings and will always love God's people.

One night I heard a message preached by Bishop Calvin Lewis; he said we had to "grow up." I thought I had grown up, but there was room for improvement. I said that night, "He is preaching to me." I was comfortable and ready to settle down in my comfort zone, but I had to grow some more.

Our God has plans and purposes for our lives, and we must obey Him. Pastors, don't get too comfortable in a place; God may say, "Move On!" He is on time, in time, and He is eternity. The timing of the Lord is a mandate. Today, I am in the timing and plans and purposes of God. No weapon formed against me shall prosper (Isaiah 54:17). There will be formable weapons, but they will not prosper! Therefore, I want to encourage pastors to obey the voice of God and have a strong spirit of discernment.

The spirit of discernment has kept me from making wrong decisions. I was angry for a moment because of some of the sheep's actions, but God gave me His unconditional love. Also, He directed me to His Word and sent me into my prayer closet. He took me off Facebook for a while and told me to write this book. I was totally delivered while I was praying, writing, reading God's Word, and meditating on Him. Therefore, I could not harm the sheep, nor could I hate them. I am a child of the King of kings and the Lord of lords. He told me to forgive and show kindness and love. "[…] with lovingkindness have I drawn thee" (Jeremiah 31:3). Furthermore, my heart goes out to pastors and sheep. We do not have to try to bring one leader down in order to promote another one. God said, "Don't give up on the sheep that have gone astray and the rebellious sheep." He will take care of them and will call them back to their first love.

I followed the instructions of God and great men and women of God. Moreover, they had experience, wisdom, the Word, and the Holy Spirit. I prayed with prayer warriors and heard the voice of God through the written word and the spoken word. Our daughter, Senior Pastor Colenthia Milner-Wright, Pastor Fagale Grant, Sister Marlene Joyce Hall, Pastor Michele Copeland, Sister Twanna Brown, Prophetess Wilma Flowers, First Lady Sadie Ellis, Pastor Juanita George-Jackson and her sisters, Pastor Alice Gipson, Apostle Kathy Taylor, Apostle Jimmie Taylor, Evangelist Rochelle Alston and her family, all of my siblings, and many others are great intercessors. They pray for my family and me. The Lord gave us preaching, praying, prophesying, teaching, and loving daughter, family, and an army of Holy Ghost-filled saints. God also placed great mentors in my life to encourage, correct, and cover me. Some of these men are Bishop Frank T. Bozeman, Pastor, Dr. Claude A. Shuford, Pastor, Dr. Walter E. Ellis, Dr. J. C. Wade, Jr., and the late moderator Clifford Thomas, late Rev. Dan Johnson (my father in ministry), late Rev. Douglas Nicholson, Sr., and Rev. James Mctier, Jr.

Finally, the Judas spirit was identified by some of the saints. This spirit must be abolished by the power of the Holy Ghost and the Word of God. Pastors must live and speak God's Word. Pastors must demonstrate God's Word through signs, wonders, and miracles. The fivefold ministry must be in operation, also the fruit of the spirit and the gifts of the spirit. The Bible says,

> These signs will follow those who believe: In
> My name they will cast out demons; they will
> speak with new tongues; they will take up ser-
> pents; and if they drink anything deadly, it will
> by no means hurt them; they will lay hands on
> the sick, and they will recover.

Mark 16:17–18 (NKJV)

During my early pastoral service, I was blessed with
five wonderful years, with the presence of my oldest brother, Pastor Humphrey L. Shuford, to come and preach our
"on fire for Jesus" crusades. He brought several ministers
with him to assist in the crusades: Pastor Dane Robinson,
our cousin, preached for one year with him. The spirit of
the Lord moved mightily in the crusade every year. Jesus
brought deliverance, salvation, restoration, and healing
and restored relationships; miracles were happening each
year. This pastor was sold out to Jesus and full of the Holy
Ghost. He identified the spirit of betrayal, the wolves in
sheep's clothing, and much more. We truly thank God for
Pastor Humphrey L. Shuford: he is an awesome, amazing,
anointed man of God. He is still preaching with profound
wisdom and prophetic insight and giving a powerful word.
Moreover, my sisters, Rev. Fagale Grant, Mrs. Marlene

Joyce Hall, and their husbands, late Rev. David L. Grant and Mr. Jesse L. Hall, Sr., are angels of mercy who God has given to me and others. I truly thank Jesus for their labor of love for my ministry and me. They are a blessing to the ministry and our family. Jesus has equipped them with the gift of help and many more.

Jesus will give pastors the people who love Him and love His servants. Again, pastors have to have a strong spirit of discernment; it is a mandate and is vital for ministry. This year in January 2021, we saw the spirit of betrayal and rebellion in full force on a national level. Saints, all of us need God's love, mercy, grace, forgiveness, correction, and chastisement. Therefore, we are praying for those unlawful individuals to be forgiven by God and man and also to be punished to the full extent of the law. They were wrong for starting a riot and invading the United States Capitol. The spirit of betrayal has to be abolished. Lord Jesus, have mercy on all of us; we need You today, tomorrow, and forever. The United States of America was invaded by angry, rebellious, ungodly, misinformed, and violent people provoked to do wrong. Some of them were American citizens and were guided in the way of the ungodly. On Wednesday, January 6, 2021, those individuals rebelled against God and their fellow citizens. Politicians, pastors, Christian leaders, and laity around the world were praying for America. We are still praying to our Lord, Jesus, to save more souls and give total deliverance to our nation. Moreover, we were in disbelief and disappointed to see these violent acts play out on national TV. Jesus, will You give all of Your children peace, forgiveness, restoration, deliverance, and reconciliation?

We saw the following three things on January 6, 2021, and much more. We saw *insurrection*, which is a noun that means "a violent uprising against an authority or government."[5] The insurrection was savagely carried out by mobsters acting like savages, acting like violent criminals, and very unpatriotic individuals. Some of them committed treason. "Treason" is a noun that means "the crime of betraying one's country, especially by attempting to kill the sovereign or overthrow the government."[6]

The mob moved into the US Capitol to overthrow the political process and destroy the pride and dignity of the democratic electoral process. The mob also displayed rebellion. "Rebellion" is a noun that means "an act of violent or open resistance to an established government or ruler."[7] The mob moved in on the USA authorities, and they were very disrespectful, violent, and rebellious.

We constantly hear 2 Chronicles 7:14. It is read, quoted, taught, and preached; it's time for God's people to obey His Word.

Lord Jesus, help us obey and live Your Word. Jesus, help all of Your pastors move in the spirit of obedience and excellence.

We need a powerful spirit of discernment. This will help pastors identify the Judas spirit and any spirit that is not of God.

CHAPTER 6

Spiritual Growth

What is spiritual growth, and why is it important to pastors, leaders, and laity?

Spiritual growth is a mandate and empowerment for all leaders. Therefore, if you have to grow in the secular arena, you must grow spiritually. In the workplace, you have to get several professional-development hours each year. If those hours are not completed each year, you are placed on probation, penalized, or, in some cases, may be terminated.

The Word of God says that newly saved individuals are fed milk; they cannot digest meat. They are spiritually "babies" and have to advance to become spiritually mature adults. The spiritual-growth process is vital for the advancement of your kingdom stewardship, your kingdom character, and your empowerment of others. Furthermore, in this virtual world that we live today, we will become obsolete, isolated, and irrelevant if we don't grow. In like manner, it is necessary for pastors and all leaders to grow spiritually in all areas of their lives. In some churches and organizations, pastors and leaders grow, but sometimes, the sheep are left behind. Pastors and leaders must make it mandatory for those in their ministry to grow in all areas. However, everyone may not grow as fast as others, but spiritual growth must be seen in them, and it must be placed as a top priority. In Hebrews 6:1–3 (MSG), the Word of God says,

> So come on, let's leave the preschool finger-painting exercises on Christ and get on with the grand work of art. Grow up in Christ. The basic foundational truths are in place, the plan salvation, turning our trust toward God, baptismal instructions, laying on of hands, resurrection of the dead, eternal judgment, and much more. With God helping us, we'll stay true to all that we need Him to help us with.

But there's so much to learn about Jesus and His assignments. I want to grow more and more each day. Let's get on with the spiritual-growth process and be elevated beyond measure. Spiritual growth has to take place in the leadership so they can lead others in the right direction. They must have goals, objectives, a strategic plan of action, timelines, and instructions from God. Pastors cannot lead the way if they don't know the way. That's why a good mentorship ministry is a great way of access to pastors and others. Pastors need others to pour into their lives as they are pouring into the sheep. Pastors have to be accountable and obey their spiritual authority in the earthly realm and obey God. Pastors and leaders show spiritual growth when they can take the advice and instructions from those in authority over them. You have not advanced spiritually in pastoral leadership if you are not teachable and submissive to your spiritual authority. On the other hand, if those in spiritual authority over you are not operating in the divine order of God, you must seek God for instructions. God will show you what to do, how to do the right thing, and when to embark upon it.

I had to grow spiritually because I wanted to grow spiritually to do an awesome job for Jesus and others. Jesus has surrounded me with great pastors, awesome leaders, excellent mentors, and protégés. The ministry road is not always smooth, but our God is always faithful. Sometimes the road gets rough, and you have to endure hardness like a good soldier. God had given me instructions, and I had to follow them. Surely, it was time to go to the next dimension in ministry. A greater spiritual-growth process had to take place in me. After you have suffered for a while, He will strengthen you, settle you, equip you, and make you perfect in Him (1 Peter 5:10). The days of growth and testing the faith had to take place for the next assignment. I have walked in faith and seen the works of faith in ministry. It was time for me to operate in the gift of faith. Therefore, I had to know that Jesus had His sheep and that they were in His hands. The question for me was: Who was watching the sheep?

We have to grow up spiritually in our position in order to be shifted to our next assignment. However, there are times when we have to move on to another position to get the needed spiritual growth. When Jesus is in charge of your ministry, He knows what's best for you. Saints, I thought I was watching the sheep and doing a good job. The five-year goals for the ministry were written, and the ten-year goals were written; some of them were being implemented. Also, I had those goals on the table of my heart.

But Jesus said, "It's time to move on!" The visions, plans, and purposes were for another phase of my ministry. Moreover, I did not know that the alignment of 2012 would shift me into a new season in my ministry for 2020. I had to go to another dimension in my spiritual growth. The pastoral assignment was a blessing and an opportunity for the sheep and me. Jesus had placed me in a ministry to serve His people.

I was at home, in the hometown where I grew up and attended school. However, the Bible clearly says that "a prophet is not without honour, but in his own country"

(Mark 6:4). I had been in ministry for twenty-seven years, in one place. Surely, I thought that Jesus would not move me from this position! Today, it is my thirty-seventh year as a minister, as a gospel preacher of Jesus Christ. Yes, I see it more clearly now: it was time to move on! Our spiritual growth comes in different ways; what I needed was not in a place of comfort. Jesus told me that I could move in two ways. They were: obeying His voice and living peacefully or dying and going to be with Jesus. I said, "Jesus, I will obey You today!" I told Jesus, "Please let me live." I wanted to see my grandchildren grow up, go to school, and finish college. On the day Jesus spoke to me, I was afraid; I moved to the place that God called me to quickly! I said, "Lord Jesus, I want to help Bishop and Prophetess Wright [our daughter] in ministry. I want to see our children and grandchildren work in ministry and serve You, Jesus. I believe our sons, TJay and Zack, will preach the gospel one day. I want to live and see them work in ministry. I truly thank You, Jesus, for giving me another chance."

My assignment was at a good church, my second-home church, Good Hope Missionary Baptist Church, Wetumpka, Alabama, where we built a new church. I love Good Hope, and I want the best for His people. There were hidden agendas and minor problems, but Jesus did not allow me to see them all. He trusted me to love, build, encourage, correct, forgive, win souls, counsel, let my light shine for Him, and do the work of a true pastor. I thank You, Jesus, for trusting me to pastor Your people, and I thank Your people for giving me the opportunity.

The spiritual-growth process takes time, and you have to endure your cross in life. When Jesus elevates you in the spirit, your work has to become greater for His kingdom! Likewise, when Saul was changed to Apostle Paul, he was given a greater work for the kingdom. Apostle Paul wrote a large portion of the New Testament!

On the day that my pastoral assignment ended at the church in Wetumpka, I was sad. Jesus said, "You have to grow up and walk as a prophet." I did not want this new assignment, but He was preparing me for it. Moreover, Jesus said, "There is a greater harvest of souls and blessings for you and your family." Also, Jesus said, "There are those who cannot advance until you move out! They are connected to your destiny."

I thought I was there to stay. *Wow*! I had to grow up spiritually. Jesus said, "No, My child, you have not arrived at your final destination. You prepared for the world and are ministering to one area. Don't be afraid; arise and obey My voice. Retire from pastoring to be free for your next assignment. You are called in this season to be a prophet.

I formed you and ordained you a prophet to the nations before you were formed in your mother's womb."

The day that I was told by Jesus to move on! He opened my spiritual eyes, and He showed me some of the deceiving spirits. I was shocked and very hurt, but I had to grow up! I said, "Lord, I thought these people loved me."

But God's ways are not our ways; God's thoughts are not our thoughts (Isaiah 55:8–9). He has plans for you and me that have to be revealed to us. The good part about my transition was (1) in order for me to grow spiritually, I had to be pushed into my destiny; (2) the hearts of some of the people had to change, and (3) I had to be healed. Therefore, I could not return back to this ministry until God released me to go. The spiritual growth that I needed, they needed as well. *Wow*! To God be the glory. Yes, saints, I cried; I hugged my daughter, husband, members, and others and said goodbye to almost forty years of my adult life in one church. Again, thirty-eight years of ministry as a preacher and the remaining years as a dedicated layperson.

When we are introduced to change, we welcome it, embrace it, ignore it, and we can reject it. In like manner, I had to embrace it and obey Jesus! Moreover, my message to pastors is to obey the voice of Jesus. He speaks to us today through the Holy Spirit. "Greater is He that is in you; than He that is in the world" (1 John 4:4). Pastors, are you in a place of comfort, are you in a transitional moment, or are you in the divine place and position that Jesus has called you to? Whatever place you are in, I say again: obey the voice of Jesus. You will be successful and shall have divine favor from God and favor from man. Likewise, remember that there will be difficult days, but you are more than a conqueror through Jesus Christ (Romans 8:37).

I obeyed Jesus; I am so glad that I did! I had to grow up spiritually in every area of my life. Some of the saints call me Hurdis, Pastor Bozeman, Sister Milner, Sister Bozeman, First Lady Bozeman, and some call me Dr. Bozeman. Yes, these are titles, but most of all, I am a servant of the Most High God, a servant leader. Jesus the Christ saved me, and He chose me. He is the Son of the living God. He chose me, qualified me, and ordained me as a prophet. I do not use the title "prophet" or "prophetess"; I use the title "Dr. Bozeman." I am not caught up in who I am! I am caught up in who Jesus is; He is my all in all.

I love You, Jesus. I worship and adore You. I just want to tell You that I love You more than anything! Therefore, thank you, Good Hope, armor-bearers, deacons, and members, for giving me a chance to be licensed and ordained and pastor you. Thank you for helping us build your new church; it was a highlight in our ministry.

The Lord gave me a great mentor, a loving husband,

a profound teacher and preacher, a true friend and bishop to help guide me through the process. I thank Dr. Frank T. Bozeman for his love, assistance, and support. Wow! I truly thank my determined, awesome, amazing, and beautiful daughter, Pastor Colenthia Milner-Wright. Our dedicated, devoted, and loyal daughter has always helped me in ministry. She is the senior pastor of Global Word Fellowship, Inc., Montgomery, Alabama, and Pastor Michele Milner-Copeland is her assistant. Pastor Milner-Wright is a powerful woman of God.

Today, and always, we will totally depend on the power of the Holy Spirit and the divine love of Jesus.

"What Love Won't Do"

Love won't take counsel against the righteous; it

will aid you in a crisis.

Love won't destroy, deplete, or dismantle you,

and hate can't get through.

Love won't kill you with foul words, deadly

weapons;

Fiery darts will not abolish your record.

Love won't see you hurting and not respond;

Some problems seem as if they weigh a ton.

Love won't lead you or leave you in a mess;

The unconditional favor of Jesus will bring out

the best.

Love from Jesus won't fail in saving your life;

Real and genuine love comes from Jesus Christ.

Love won't fill your spirit with hate;

Those who walk by faith know how to wait.

Love won't stand by and not speak what's right;

Jesus has already won the fight.

The love of Jesus is unconditional: "While we were yet sinners, Christ died for us" (Romans 5:8). Thank You, Jesus, for loving us and surrounding us with Your unfailing and abiding love.

On January 13, 2004, Jesus gave me a prophecy from Prophetess Elaine Bronson of Delaware. The woman of God said, "Seek Jesus's face. You will be traveling very much. Churches may come against you because of the work God has given you. You are different, and they don't understand you. He will show you how to prepare and study. Much of His glory, much of His riches. There is much word around you; don't worry when He calls you home; He is with you. You have lifted many burdens. You will write twelve books; some of them will be manuals.

They will include testing on knowledge and understanding, gifts of healing, and understanding His power. He is bringing you into newness all around you. Jesus says He loves you so much that you were destined for His glory.

Truly, I thank God for His divine love, favor, and blessings. Likewise, I thank Him for letting me know that He is with me and that His blood has me covered. Furthermore, there were those in ministry who were struggling, and they wanted to hear from God but were reluctant to get help. These individuals thought they were in a place of comfort, but God gave them a prophetic shift. They had to move from their comfort zone into their present destiny.

When God shifted me from the office of a pastor to the office of a prophet, I had to go to another dimension. I was uncomfortable, uneasy, and unusual things were happening in my life. I was determined to hold on to Jesus, hold my head up, and keep the faith. Moreover, I had to grow up spiritually and walk in the prophetic assignment that God had given me. I am walking in my God-given assignment with confidence, assurance, and faith.

In Dr. Mike Murdock's email, he said,

> Give yourself enough time to achieve your goal. Good things take effort and time. Be honest with yourself concerning your talent, time, and resources. Focus only on those tasks

that you feel worthy of your total attention and time. Stress…is a chosen path. Sometimes the reward is not worth the burden.[8]

Therefore, I had to give all my agendas to Jesus and surrender all of me to Him. All things happen in the timing of the Lord. Here I am, Jesus, holy and available; use me, Lord!

The number one thing that I had to do for this assignment was to surrender to Jesus. The next dimension of my spiritual growth depended on my submitting totally to Him. The God-given assignments in ministry are necessary for producing spiritual growth. I thought that my final assignment was in Good Hope. However, I will remain faithful to Him until God calls me to my eternal heavenly home. In like manner, when God is speaking to us, we must listen, comprehend, and follow His instructions. God told me when I was given the pastoral assignment that He was placing me there for a season. Therefore, it is imperative that pastors are sensitive to the Holy Spirit. We must hear His voice and obey Him. I would rather obey God than obey man." Pastors, if you are in a decision-making process or a spiritual shift and you need help, seek Jesus!

This Is a Prayer for Pastors

Jesus, I come today with an open mind and an open heart. You are my light, my directions, and my life. I want to hear Your word clearly and obey Your word. The spiritual shift that has occurred in my life is welcomed. I am ready for Your divine change, plans, and purposes. Lord Jesus, I surrender all to You. Forgive me for not obeying You sooner. This day, Lord, I am ready to pursue my next assignment with power and purity. Jesus, thank You for helping me and trusting me to walk worthy of my calling. Thank You for covering me with the blood.

Spiritual growth, for all of those in the fivefold ministry and those in the laity, is a mandate. Lao Tzu said, "The journey of 1,000 miles begins with one step." Moreover, in Lao Tzu's quote, he was trying to express that great things start from humble beginnings. Also, in the original text, it refers to the "1,000 *li* journey." A *li* is an old Chinese measure of distance that converts to 360 miles or 576 km.

It is necessary for us to grow in all areas of our lives, but it's a process. We cannot rush the process; we have to take one step at a time. Remember that our entire journey begins with one step. In Psalm 37:23, the Bible says that "the steps of a good man are ordered by the LORD: and he delighteth in his way." The spiritual-growth process is challenging, and it changes, but when God orders your steps, you will stay on the right path.

CHAPTER 7

It's Time to Move On

In the Bible and in society today, there are many men and women of God whom God has instructed to move on. Their assignments in a particular place, region, or country have expired. Today, there are a lot of pastors and leaders who are given a mandate by God to move on. Some people obey Him, and some of them ignore His voice. On the other hand, there are some pastors and leaders instructed to wait for a while and not to make their moves too soon.

The spiritual shift of a continent, a nation, a state, a town, a city, a community, a church, a family, or an individual can be dramatic. However, it can be very rewarding. Moreover, some people are ready to move, and some are not going to move on; change is not embraced by everyone. They will not hear, nor will they obey the voice of God.

Moses had to leave the pharaoh's house and live in the desert. Abraham obeyed God and left his kindred. Ruth left her people and went with her mother-in-law. Peter and Andrew put down their nets and followed Jesus. Mary

Magdalene got delivered of seven devils, and she followed Jesus. How many pastors and leaders are working today obediently, willing to get delivered and set free, and following Jesus? I truly believe that we are willing and ready to follow Jesus. When I speak of following Jesus, I mean that you will drop what you are doing and move to another city, state, town, country, etc. Will pastors be willing to pack their bags, say farewell to a church and a community of people that they love, and move on? Listen: it's easy to say, but it's harder to do. It took me three years to move on; I wanted to stay and finish my plan, but it was not God's plan for my life at that hour.

Moreover, you may have a good plan with all the things in order in the natural, but God may say, "No, it's not My will for you in this season." Pastors obey His voice. They lead His sheep; they preach, teach His Word, live His Word, and give the three *T*s: their time, their talent, and their tithes, but some of them and some of their members don't welcome and embrace change. Sometimes, in order to fulfill the plans of God for the ministry, change has to take place in various areas of our lives. You may be doing a great job; you may be involved in various projects; you may be the pastor of the year, but you are not in spiritual alignment. Pastors walking the walk and talking the talk but not obeying the voice of God have to obey His voice.

God told them to move on, and some of them said, "Lord, I can't do it." Some may be saying, "Send someone else; I am tired of building up what others have messed up." God doesn't count His chosen pastors out. His chosen leaders are given another chance because God is faithful and just; He will cleanse us from all sin and unrighteousness. Therefore, God gives us more than one chance; He is not like man.

If I had the knowledge years ago of what I have knowledge of now, I would not have been hurt, misused, and crying like a mistreated pastor. I would have moved into my destiny joyously, with perseverance and tenacity. I was sold out to Jesus a long time ago because He is the only one who truly understands everything about me. Thank You, Jesus! I am thankful that Jesus has made me sincere, serious, sanctified, and strong in the Lord. But I still need help from others, and there are others who need my help. We will continue to lift pastors up in prayer, encourage them, and bless them; I feel their cries sometimes.

Some of the saints will say they don't know why their pastors are not willing to compromise. Truly, sold-out pastors and leaders do not compromise with man; they follow the voice of God and walk in complete obedience. However, before they pass judgment on any individual, they will seek God for His instructions. He knows all things and sees everything: Why not ask God instead of asking man? When a pastor's decision is not what people want to hear, sometimes the people will say that the pastor is wrong. Pastors, I see and hear your cries; hold on.

On the other hand, they may say the pastor needs to go back to the altar because they did not hear from God. When it's time to move on, a pastor will have many people coming their way with misguided and misleading information. Also, there will be those who have heard from God, and they understand their pastor, pray for them, encourage them, and give an offering to them. However, the pastor must follow God's directions and move forward in the way of the Lord.

How many times in the Bible did God allow the sheep to lead the shepherd? People are instructed to help the pastor work the God-given vision. God will give the provisions, keep His promises to the pastor, and validate His plans. We cannot look to see a vision come to fruition all at once. The pastor and the people have to wait on God's instructions and timing. They have to trust God for everything!

We can trust Jesus for a pastor to help build a church, marry our children, officiate at the homegoing of our family, counsel us, pray for us, and give us a divine word. But some of the saints do not trust their pastor to move into new kingdom assignments. Oh yes, think about it and let Jesus's light shine on you, in you, and through you. The Lord is sovereign, and He does what He wants to do. He has our lives in His hands; He is the Alpha and Omega. His grace is sufficient for us, and His strength is made perfect in our weakness (2 Corinthians 12:9). Listen: Jonah did not want to go to his next assignment, and he got in a bad situation. Jonah 2:1–4 reads:

> Then Jonah prayed unto the LORD his God out of the fish's belly, And said, I cried by reason of mine affliction unto the LORD, and he heard me; out of the belly of hell cried I, and thou hearest my voice for thou hadst cast me into the deep, in the midst of the seas; and the floods compassed me about: all thy billows and thy waves passed over me. Then I said, I am cast out of thy sight; yet I will look again toward thy holy temple.

Jonah messed up the plan and instructions that God had given him, but when Jonah prayed, cried out to God, and repented, God brought deliverance to Jonah. In like manner, there are pastors and leaders running away from their God-given assignments instead of running to them. When it's time to move on to the next assignment, the pastor will know because God will give them directions.

The Lord Jesus will be with you even until the end of the world. The Lord will show you visions, give you dreams, prophetic insight, revelation knowledge, a word of wisdom, a word of knowledge, and many other signs when it's time to move on.

Moreover, I remember when it was time for me to leave my secular job and the church that I was assigned to; it was a struggle every time that I had to go there. When I would get near the places, my spirit would be troubled. I knew that I had to move on, but my flesh wanted to stay. My spirit wanted me to obey and receive the guidance of the Holy Spirit.

In Ruth 1:16, she said, "Intreat me not to leave thee, or to return from following after thee: for whither thou goest, I will go; and where thou lodgest, I will lodge: thy people shall be my people, and thy God my God." Ruth knew that it was time for a change in her life and that she had to go with her mother-in-law to another place. Therefore, Ruth went with Naomi, and her life was productive. Ruth walked with her, talked with her, and obeyed Naomi. Naomi and Ruth trusted their God for the provisions, the plan, the process, and His promises. Glory to God! They knew how to trust God. Therefore, pastors, leaders, and laity must trust God's plans, purposes, provisions, and promises. When God says, "Move on," move quickly, assured, with faith and confidence.

When it was time for Peter and Andrew, two of Jesus's disciples, to move on, they dropped their nets and followed Jesus. It's time for some of the pastors and leaders to drop what they are doing and move into a new realm with Jesus. They may have nets (problems) that are tied to wrong relationships, careers, past disappointments, abuse, grief, the pandemic, economic hardship, or a lack of faith. Whatever their problems are, Jesus is the ultimate answer. The disciples had to encounter many situations before they truly learned that Jesus had all the answers to their problems. Moreover, it is said that it took two boats to take the catch back to shore when Jesus told His disciples to launch out into the deep. Luke 5:4–6 says,

> Now when he had left speaking, he said unto Simon, Launch out into the deep, and let down your nets for a draught. And Simon answering said unto him, Master, we have toiled all night, and have taken nothing: nevertheless at thy word I will let down the net. And when they had this done, they enclosed a great multitude of fishes: and their net brake.

In like manner, we have to move from the shallow waters of life and launch out into the deep. When it's time to transition from one place to another, pastors and leaders have to say, "Nevertheless, but at Thy word Jesus, I will move on." The miracle in Luke, chapter five, started with one small step of obedience against all odds. The disciples followed the voice of Jesus and received a great miracle. How long will it take for some of the men and women of God to obey the voice of Jesus? I am ashamed to say that it took me three years to move on. The awesome thing about my moving on later is that Jesus's grace is sufficient for me; His strength is made perfect in my weakness.

Don't allow doubt, mistakes, disappointments, delay, discouragement, or denial to abort your destiny of freedom and advancement in the kingdom. Move on and watch God move you into a mighty, better, and life-changing experience. Move on, speak, decree, and declare that it's already done!

"Move On"

Move on if God said so; don't look back.

Obedience to His word will keep you on track.

Oh yes, God said it without a shadow of a doubt.

He is all-powerful and all-knowing; surely, He

will bring you out.

Don't look to man, nor to the left or to the right.

Our Lord and our Savior will always bring you
out.

Stop being afraid to move by what God has said.

You have His angels watching over you,

And with the Holy Spirit, you shall be led.

Pastor, I heard your cries, and they have reached
beyond the sky.

Jesus is interceding for you; He is always and
forever right,

Listening to your heartbeats and seeing the frowns
on your face.

You have to let it go and depend on His sweet
amazing grace.

Today, I will continue to look to Jesus for you and
for me.

Pastors, I know that our Lord will soon set you
free.

In His loving arms, you can rest and be at peace.

The days of testing and trials will allow you

To move on and get sweet relief.

CHAPTER 8

Embracing Life's Challenges

Pastors and leaders have so many critical conditions, crises, and circumstances on a daily basis. Some of the dilemmas cannot be taken care of without God's help. In the Bible, it said: "Jehoshaphat, Thus saith the LORD unto you, Be not afraid nor dismayed by reason of this great multitude; for the battle is not yours, but God's" (2 Chronicles 20:15). Some battles are not for pastors and leaders to fight; they are God's battles. Therefore, when pastors and leaders realize that they are not called or chosen to fix everything or take care of everybody's issues, their lives become less stressful.

In my pastoral role, I surrender totally to Jesus. All the issues that were not assigned for me to take care of, I gave to God. People will demand from you more than you are capable of handling. There is an old saying: "you can't get blood out of a turnip." I say you can't get milk out of an empty glass. The question is: What does the Lord require of you? The minor prophet Micah states some vital requirements of God in Micah 6:6–8:

Wherewith shall I come before the LORD, and bow myself before the high God? shall I come before him with burnt offerings, with calves of a year old? Will the LORD be pleased with thousands of rams, or with ten thousands of rivers of oil? shall I give my firstborn for my transgression, the fruit of my body for the sin of my soul? He hath shewed thee, O man, what is good; and what doth the LORD require of thee, but to do justly, and to love mercy, and to walk humbly with thy God?

There are so many pastors and leaders trying to produce in areas that they were not assigned by God, and they are having multiple issues. It's a great thing when we operate in our God-given assignments and know what God requires of us. If you are reading this book and feel that you are out of place, stop right now and pray to Jesus for His divine guidance. In Proverbs 3:5–6, it is said: "Trust in the LORD with all thine heart; and lean not unto thine own understanding. In all thy ways acknowledge him, and he shall direct thy paths." Truly, Jesus is a path director and a problem solver. You have to seek Him and acknowledge Him in everything that you do. His ways are not like our ways. Isaiah 55:8–9 says,

For my thoughts are not your thoughts, neither

are your ways my ways, saith the LORD. For as
the heavens are higher than the earth, so are my
ways higher than your ways, and my thoughts
than your thoughts.

The year 2020 has brought so much hardship, pain, and challenges to pastors, leaders, the body of Christ, and the entire world. Some of the pastors and the churches were not prepared for the present-day ministry style. The social-media community has played a vital role in the lives of pastors, leaders, churches, schools, and most of our society. The social-media world is frightening to some pastors and leaders. It has caused stress for so many of them. My heart goes out to our pastors and leaders because you can see and hear their cries. I had to cry in the past because of mistreatments, disappointments, and so many other critiques and crises, but the blood of Jesus prevailed. I decree right now in the mighty name of Jesus that the blood of Jesus shall prevail! Moreover, the cries of pastors from all over the world shall be heard, and they shall be attended to in a timely manner.

On the other hand, don't forget that pastors have a private life and a public life, and we must respect that. They cannot move mountains all over the world. They have to take the assignments that God gives them and work those assignments according to how God has ordered them. You cannot expect pastors to work miracles; Jesus is the miracle worker. He works His miracles through pastors and others. Some pastors and some of our leaders have placed too much on themselves. Jesus's burdens are light. Matthew tells us in Matthew 11:28–30:

> Come unto me, all ye that labour and are heavy laden, and I will give you rest. Take my yoke upon you, and learn of me; for I am meek and lowly in heart: and ye shall find rest unto your souls. For my yoke is easy, and my burden is light.

Jesus has not put these heavy burdens on us. Some of our pastors and leaders have allowed people to place restraints and restrictions on them. However, some of them have placed restraints and restrictions on themselves. These heavy burdens are like heavy metal hanging around their necks. Pastors and leaders need to be free and operate in the spirit of liberty in their private and public lives. It's difficult for some pastors and leaders right now during this pandemic. They encounter so many with physical, spiritual, social, emotional, and economic needs. There are not enough resources in some areas to give aid to families and churches. This makes pastors cry out to Jesus even more and seek help for their families and churches. The cries have been heard by God, and He is releasing His angels on the pastors' behalf.

The workload can be overwhelming and draining for pastors at times, but they have to continue to fight the good fight of faith and trust God for everything. Pastors can be transparent in some areas of their lives, but they cannot allow people to share in some of the things that they are dealing with. People cannot handle some of the problems and circumstances that pastors and leaders have to deal with. Pastors are crying late in the midnight hours, early in the morning, at noonday, and throughout the day. The prayers of some of our pastors are going up right now!

May Jesus continue to bless, protect, cover with His blood, instruct, lead, and guide His pastors!

I am in a family full of pastors and those in the fivefold ministry. My mother, late Rev. Cora Rebecca Crenshaw Shuford, and my sister, late Pastor Charlena Shuford-Miller, were awesome, anointed, amazing, powerful, profound, and prophetic preachers of the gospel. God poured out a mighty anointing on these two ladies, and they ministered to so many before God called them home. I will always remember their labor of love, their wisdom, knowledge, integrity, and the incredible witnesses that they were in the earthly realm. Yes, pastors cry and deal with hideous things, crucial circumstances, and adverse conditions, but they can look to the hill of help twenty-four seven; Jesus is the answer to every question and problem.

CHAPTER 9

The Anointing Doesn't Come Cheap

By Jeremia H. Milner (my granddaughter):

Some saints use this phrase often: "I am not going to pay this amount for these items." Sometimes, they will say these items are too much out-of-pocket cost: "You can put that one back on the shelf; I can't buy it right now." Saints know how to shop thriftily, how to shop economically, and they know how to shop extravagantly. Also, they will show you where the extravagant, thrifty, and elegant stores are located. Some of the saints know how to shop wisely, and others—wastefully. It's nothing wrong with the saints shopping when they shop wisely.

Some things in life don't come cheap: you have to be prepared to invest in the things that you need. In like manner, there are people willing to drive miles to save two dollars without considering the fact that the gas costs much more. Some people shop on the internet to find the least expensive and the most expensive items. Sometimes, they have to pay more in order to get the best unless there are special deals and discounts.

Let's think about this from a spiritual perspective and allow it to get your attention. I was wondering: How do you shop when you want something from God? This is a good question for all Christians to ask themselves. Yes, ask yourself this question and answer it truthfully. Saints, do you ask Jesus for something and try to get the cheapest blessing? Do you say, "Jesus, just give me the economy and the thrifty spiritual things"? On the other hand, do you try to get a quick fix and the easy way out?

I am thinking about spiritual shopping and getting the best from Jesus. Just as you want the best from Jesus, you should give Him your best. Therefore, all of us need to give Jesus our best, and we shouldn't give Him any leftovers. We want Him to give us His best. He deserves the best praise, worship, prayers, tithes, and offerings. Everything that we give to Jesus should be our best.

When we shop physically and spiritually, we want the best. Saints, when Jesus gives us His blessings, He does not give us His leftovers; He gives us the best. He has done so much for us that we cannot tell it all. We all have to shop wisely when we shop physically and spiritually. There are things that are not for us, and there are things that we don't need or want.

It's a blessing to go through storms knowing that you have given Jesus your best. Moreover, it is when we give

Jesus our best that we will come out with more of Jesus's anointing. We must live by the Word; Jesus is the Word made flesh. We cannot just be hearers of the Word; we must be hearers and doers of His Word. Therefore, shop in His Word and get the things that you need daily. The Bible tells us in John 1:13–14 (NKJV), "Who were born not of blood, nor [...] of the will of man but of God. And the word became flesh and dwelt among us, and we beheld His glory, as of the only begotten of the Father, full of grace and truth." Jesus is full of grace and truth; you can shop in His Word, always coming out richer. Our Lord and Savior had to pay the price in the wilderness, fasting and praying for forty days and forty nights. The anointing did not come cheap in His natural life. Therefore, after the forty days and forty nights of fasting and praying, Jesus began His public ministry.

He is Jesus Christ, the Anointed One. Jesus paid the ultimate price for our sins at Calvary. He shed His precious blood for our sins. Matthew 4:17 (NKJV) tells us, "From that time Jesus began to preach and to say, 'Repent, for the kingdom of heaven is at hand.'"

The anointing did not come cheap in the life of Jesus, and it does not come cheap in the lives of preachers and laity. They all have suffered to receive the anointing that is yoke destroying, burden removing, power packed, and healing. They have weathered the storms of life with the help of Jesus. Isaiah 61:1 (NKJV) tells us,

> The Spirit of the Lord God is upon me, because the Lord has anointed me to preach good tidings to the poor; He has anointed me to heal the brokenhearted, to proclaim liberty to the captives, and the opening of the prison to those who are blind.

Jesus received this anointing and worked His public ministry with an abundance of power. Jesus was 100 percent God and 100 percent man. When Jesus was at Calvary, He paid the price for our salvation, anointing, healing, and for us to have eternal life. He rose on the third day in the morning with explosive earthquake-like anointing power. Jesus has given this power to His children. We have *dunamis* power (dynamite power) that was given to us by Jesus.

In like manner, there are several other family members, leaders, sons, and daughters in ministry to who I dedicate the book. Jeremia and I give special acknowledgments to our spiritual leaders and mentors.

Let's stop, look, and listen to the meaning of the word "anointing." The word "anointing" comes from the root word "anoint." The Oxford online dictionary says that the word "anoint" is a verb (with an object), meaning to "ceremonially confer divine or holy office or power"[9] upon someone who has been chosen for this particular office or task. Moreover, the origin of the word "anoint" is in Middle English, from the Old French *enoint* "anointed," past participle of *enoindre*. According to Webster Dictionary Online, the word "anoint" means to "smear with liquid," "apply oil," "rub," or "sprinkle."[10] Also, it means to "consecrate" or "make sacred" in a ceremony that includes the applying of oil.

In Psalm 23:5 (NKJV), David said: "You prepare a table before me in the presence of my enemies; you anoint my head with oil; my cup runs over." David, a shepherd boy, became the king of Israel. He had to pay the price for this precious anointing. Therefore, David's anointing did not come cheap. He had to run, hide, and fight Saul and his army, but God prevailed. The office of the king brought David the death of his firstborn child by Beersheba. David had a son named Absalom, who rebelled against him. Yes, David had to pay dearly for his anointing.

We all have to seek more of Jesus's anointing. We will experience some dangerous situations, some setbacks, and some storms of life, but Jesus will cover us with His blood.

The setbacks and the storms of life produce greater comebacks. Leaders, obey God! The vicissitudes of life will help bring our destiny to the place that God ordered. When we have storms in our lives, we can count it all joy. James 1:2–4 tells us to count it all joy when we fall into diverse temptations, knowing that the testing of our faith produces patience. But we have to let patience have its perfect work so that we may be perfect and complete, lacking nothing.

Furthermore, my personal testimonies have pressed Jesus's anointing in me day by day, month by month, and year by year. He has done so much for me that I cannot tell it all. Truly, we have found out that Jesus is a friend who will stick closer than a brother (Proverbs 18:24). The anointing has enlightened and empowered my assignments every second, every minute, and every hour of the day. We can't do the work of the ministry without Jesus's anointing. When changes come, leaders have to alter their prayer lives, intensify praise and worship, and increase their fasting. Moreover, when leaders notice a change and new beginnings, they must plead the blood of Jesus and stay in His Word. The change that God gives us is good for our lives; we must keep the faith and hold on.

The Leaders' Prayer

Lord Jesus, have mercy upon us and forgive us of our sins. Thank You for Your everlasting love and mercy.

I am praying this leaders' prayer, believing that pastors are covered with the blood of Jesus. Your pastors are blessed and highly favored.

All of the pastors' needs are met because of Your Word and the promises that You have given in it. Jesus, help Your children forgive others who have transgressed against them. Thank You, Jesus, for Your divine wisdom, knowledge, guidance, understanding, peace, and discernment. Help Your pastors continue to obey Your Word, serve You, reverence You, and walk in Your ways and will. Thank You, Jesus, for giving pastors another chance to change their plans to the Master's plan. "For I know the thoughts that I think toward you, saith the LORD, thoughts of peace, and not of evil, to give you an expected end" (Jeremiah 29:11).

Amen!

Worship Songs Written by Jeremia H. Milner

January 12, 2011

"As Humble as I Can"

Verse 1

Endow me, and feel me, guide me,

And lead me the right way.

I need Thee, oh! I need Thee! Yes, I do.

Chorus

For I come to You as humble as I can!

For I come to You as humble as I can!

I come broken, busted, and disgusted, but God,

  I come…

Yeah, knees bowed, and arms stretched out,

But God, I come.

For I come to You as humble as I can.

Verse 2

Lord, carry me and bless me.

Teach me to obey, obey Your Word.

Live in me so they will see Christ…

I need Thee, oh! I need Thee! Yes, I do.

Chorus

For I come to You as humble as I can!

For I come to You as humble as I can!

I come broken, busted, and disgusted, but God,

  I come…

Yeah, knees bowed, and arms stretched out,

But God, I come.

For I come to You as humble as I can.

Bridge

For I come to You as humble as I can. × 8

"Worship"

Verse 1

There is stillness in the air; Your presence fills this place.

The anointing is wavering, and it's surrounding me with a glow from above.

Shower me with Your sweet perfume and with Your blood.

I'll forever worship You.

Chorus

I Worship You! × 3

I worship You with my whole heart.

I Worship You! × 3

I worship with a song of You.

Verse 2

King of kings and Lord of lords,

The controller of life,

You're an awesome God, mighty and victorious.

I seek Your face day by day.

I surrender all, and I sacrifice my life to

Thee, O God. I'll forever worship You.

Chorus

I Worship You! × 3

I worship You with my whole heart.

I Worship You! × 3

I worship with a song of You.

Bridge

I worship You in spirit and in truth.

I worship; I worship You; I just worship You.

I lift hands and worship Him; I give my life so I

　　worship

Only Him. Come on and help me,

Help me worship Him.

I worship You with my whole heart, Jesus. × 4

The anointing doesn't come cheap—I am a living witness to the fact. It's true and has been proven over and over again.

CHAPTER 10

A Place of Peace

What is peace to the saints when they are going through a storm?

What is peace to a busy pastor? Sometimes, a pastor has to minister at a funeral, leave the gravesite at 1:00 p.m., and go to perform a wedding at 2:00 p.m. Jesus is our peace in the midst of adverse circumstances and in pleasant conditions. He keeps you in your right mind so you can serve in peace. The Merriam-Webster Dictionary states that the word "peace" can mean several things. It can mean the "state of tranquility or quietness." On the other hand, peace is "freedom from disquieting or oppressive thoughts or emotions." Also, "peace" can mean a "pact or agreement to end hostilities between those who have been at war, or in a state of enmity."[11]

The Bible says in Philippians 4:7 that He will give us peace that surpasses all understanding. Peace is a state of harmony characterized by the lack of violent conflict. It is tranquility, calmness, ease, and absence of stress. The book of Psalms has a variety of verses that give us hope, peace, praise, worship, thanksgiving, and joy. In Psalm 51:10, King David needed inner cleansing and forgiveness. He wrote, "Create in me a clean heart, O God, and renew the right spirit within me."

Pastors need the peace that flows like a river, and some of them need Jesus to cleanse them. I needed this peace when Jesus shifted me into my next kingdom assignment. I was a pastor after God's own heart, and I wanted to serve His people longer. I was in my comfort zone and did not want to move. When my time was up, I was not at peace for the first two months. However, one day, Jesus gave me a release in my spirit, and I received His peace. The peace of God that man cannot understand came over me and within me. I was on my way to healing, blessings, and my new kingdom assignment.

When pastors after God's own heart get inner peace, He gives them their sweet rest. When we get Jesus's peace, we learn how to rest in the Lord, as Psalm 37:7 tells us. Jesus is our peace. Jesus will aid His children and give them peace and the necessary tools for ministry. He knows that the pastor needs:

1. *Insight*, which means "the understanding of a specific cause and effect in a specific context"; "a piece of information or the understanding of the inner nature of things or seeing intuitively."[12] In

Greek, it's called *noesis.*

2. *Instructions,* which means "teaching or giving directions or directives; imparting knowledge and information."

3. *Increase,* which means "to become greater in size, amount, intensity, or degree. An instance of growing or making greater."[13]

Wow! I was so glad to receive His inner peace. I know that there are pastors who are reading this book right now and saying, "Lord, thank You for Your peace." In my place of peace, Jesus gave me greater insight into my kingdom assignment. He gave me an increase in various areas of my life. His anointing was given to me in a greater way. I am so thankful for my new kingdom assignment. Therefore, I am growing more in Him, writing books, finishing long-overdue projects, and giving Him all the praise. Jesus got me out of my comfort zone and gave me greater insight, His divine instructions, and much increase. Hallelujah, Jesus! The move of God in my life has been a blessing. In like manner, there were areas of spiritual growth that I needed to receive, and I could not get in my comfort zone. Some things do not grow in all types of soil, and it is necessary to plant them in another soil. Yes, what Jesus had for me was not to be planted where I was, but during the next kingdom assignment, I had to plant it there.

The peace in this place of ministry is awesome! There is a place in Jesus where I love to be, and in that place, there are:

- Pleasures forevermore!
- In Psalm 16:11 (NKJV), the Bible says: "You will show me the path of life; in your presence is the fullness of joy; at your right hand are pleasures forevermore."
- I can truly say that it is a place of peace, and you can rest in the Lord! In Psalm 37:7, the Bible says: "Rest in the LORD, and wait patiently for Him: fret not thyself because of him who prospereth in His way, because of the man who bringeth wicked devices to pass."

Pastors, we don't have to worry about man; rest in the Lord. The Bible says in Romans 12:19, "Dearly beloved, avenge not yourselves, but rather give place unto wrath: for it is written, Vengeance is Mine, I will repay, saith the Lord." Jesus gave me permanent peace. He does not give us a temporary fix.

Pastors, let Jesus take care of man, and let yourselves rest in the Lord. Likewise, when the Prince of peace, Jehovah Shalom, comes and fills pastors, they live with peace, and they can rest in Him. He gives His pastors and the saints "joy unspeakable and full of glory."[14]

The cries of pastors are going forth every day. Do you hear your pastor's cry? Some of the cries are prayers for saints, sinners, and their families. However, some of the cries are of hurt, pain, disappointment, need, and cries for help! Therefore, as saints, you have to be more sensitive to the needs and cries of pastors. Someone may say, "You are not talking to me." I may not be talking to you, but you know someone who needs this message. Will you share it with them?

Pastors are faced with challenges of their own: with their family, flock, on their job, in their communities, state, nation, and some pastors are world leaders. Let's pray for pastors and help them with their kingdom assignment. In like manner, prayer warriors and intercessors must help pastors with spiritual warfare. They must not contribute to the problems but help alleviate them.

Furthermore, you can intercede for the pastor's family and their staff. There is a great need for true intercession in church: the cries of pastors are heard in the spirit by true intercessors. The cries of pastors are heard in the spirit of love, joy, inner peace, and faith. The new kingdom assignment from Jesus will be rewarding and productive because the prayers have produced breakthroughs. All the prayers, cries, and seeking Jesus have paid off. The Bible says, "The effectual fervent prayers of a righteous man availeth much" (James 5:16).

"Much prayer, much power, little prayer, little power. No prayer, no power."[15] Prayer will help produce peace and power. A place of peace is where all pastors want to be. In this place of peace, pastors can hear from God and receive His instructions.

A Tribute to My Husband, Late Bishop,

Dr. Frank T. Bozeman

Last year was the forty-third year in ministry for Bishop Frank T. Bozeman. I wrote this tribute for him on Sunday, August 30, 2020:

Congratulations to Bishop, Dr. Frank T. Bozeman, who is celebrating his forty-third year in ministry. He has released two new CD singles this year: one in April, *He Brought Me Through*, and one in July, titled *You Can't Block My Blessings*.

Also, the bishop has coauthored two new books: *It's Personal* and *It's Personal 2*. He has been preaching and teaching the gospel of Jesus Christ for a long time. The bishop was called to preach in August 1978, and he was licensed by his spiritual father, Dr. J. C. Wade, Jr., at Zion Missionary Baptist Church, East Chicago, Indiana.

Moreover, as he reflects back on how God has blessed and favored him, he can't help but say, "Thank You, Lord

Jesus." He has preached through the storms of life. He has prayed and sung his way out of conflict with confidence in Jesus and courage to conquer many battles.

We are praying for his recovery and restoration right now. Bishop Bozeman has endured hardness like a good soldier; he suffered a stroke in 1998 while preaching, but God brought him out. In like manner, he had suffered kidney disease and many vicissitudes of life, but he continues to preach God's Word.

When you are called, chosen, chastened, and face life challenges, you have to trust Jesus for everything. Furthermore, we truly thank Jesus for our presiding bishop of Global Word Fellowship, Inc., for his labor of love for the body of Christ. May Jesus continue to overtake Bishop, Dr. Frank T. Bozeman with His richest blessings and favor. We love you, bishop.

In the Bible, King David said,

> [Lord] you have turned for me my mourning into dancing; you have put off my sackcloth and clothed me with gladness. To the end that my glory may sing praises to you and not be silent. O Lord my God, I will give thanks to you forever.

Psalm 30:11–12 (NKJV)

Bishop Bozeman, pastors, and saints, Jesus will give you His peace in the midst of a storm.

We pray that this testimonial book will bless pastors across the land and the sea. May Jesus continue to give His pastors a place of peace. May the blessings of the Lord continue to overtake you in the mighty name of Jesus!

"He Is the Lord"

Jesus is the Lord of our lives.

He is our source and our guide.

Jesus is in the midst of the storm.

His love and power make us strong.

When we are burdened, sick, or sad,

Jesus's Word will make us glad.

He will always provide.

Jesus will cause the stormy winds to subside.

Don't fight the task; just listen and obey.

The Lord will teach you a greater way.

He is still working on you.

Stand up, smile, and shout. Jesus will see you
    through.

We want to receive another touch.

Jesus Christ is willing to give you so much.

Today was a day of testing like never before.

The Word has promises that will give you His

overflow.

To Jesus, my offering I will bring.

He gives me melodies in my heart to sing.

Jesus is the Lord of lords and the King of kings.

He will carry you through everything.

Oh yes, Jesus will carry His pastors and leaders through. He is omniscient, omnipotent, and omnipresent. Jesus is able to do more than we can ask or think. The poem below speaks about Jesus being able to do everything that we need.

"He Is Able"

He is able to make you feel brand-new: have no

fear.

Stop crying, don't sweat, child: Jesus is near.

He has seen you in a distracted and puzzling

dream.

You know that His children are loving and kind,

not mean.

Your prayers have been answered, and yes, Jesus

says that He has granted.

Jesus is blessing you beyond measure; my child,

don't you panic.

The days of trials, testing, and difficulty will

cease.

You just keep doing right and believing; you will

see an increase.

When you give it all to Jesus and truly pray,

Your Lord and Savior will certainly make a way.

Just turn everything over to Jesus; you are going

to be all right.

He is able to do all things; you just cling to Him

real tight.

The cries, heartaches, overwhelming circumstances, and pain pushed me into another dimension of faith. After all that we had been through as servant leaders, pastors, bishops, and educators, there were greater dimensions to encounter. Yes, Jesus had given us a place of peace, but the greatest tests of all had to come. Our Facebook post on October 2, 2020, read as follows: "The bishop said, 'I won't complain, I am trusting God.'" I have been in the hospital for sixty-four days and still counting down the days in the rehabilitation hospital. I will be there for 14–21 days. I never wish this journey on anyone.

In the year 2021, the bishop had to endure hardship like a good soldier again. He spent forty-five more days in the hospital and the rehabilitation center. We have seen more miracles, and our faith has escalated. During the days, weeks, and months of testing, I saw miracle after miracle! The professional medical staff was excellent, the medical-assistance teams were good, the prayer warriors, our pastor, first lady, father in ministry, and our spiritual mother were phenomenal. Our family and friends around the globe are awesome. Revelatory knowledge, prophetic empowerment, grace, mercy, favor, healing, deliverance, and restoration are working in our lives. The preparation and new beginnings for Bishop Frank T. Bozeman were beyond measure.

Jesus had done it again: he raised the man of God from his sickbed for over a year. The bishop was given time to finish some major projects before going to glory. Moreover, we had many days when he had to cry with the members, friends, and others as they were experiencing various dilemmas. He pastored eight churches and served as a presiding bishop from 2006 to 2021; to God be the glory.

This time it was us crying out to Jesus for help: my dear husband was leaving this life on the earth to go to eternal life. Jesus heard our cries and delivered, healed, and made him whole. Bishop Frank T. Bozeman fought a good fight, kept the faith, and received his heavenly reward on November 20, 2021. I cannot tell it all, nor can I write it all.

Yes, pastors and leaders cry and go through the valley of the shadow of death, but they have the Shepherd of all sheep on their side. I wrote the poem below when my husband, Bishop Frank T. Bozeman, was doing better; he stayed for over 109 days in the hospital within a year and three months. This was his most extended stay before God called him to his eternal home.

The Lord spoke, and we received His commission.

"The Lord Jesus Has Spoken"

> The Lord Jesus has spoken, and we have heard
> His Word.
> He sits high and looks down low to feed the little
> bird.
> His healing hands are moving all across the land.
> His promises and His mercy are in the Master's
> plan.

The pains and the affliction of the righteous, He
has already seen.

Sometimes, we look at life circumstances as
frustrating dreams.

The right timing of the Lord Jesus will surely
come into clear sight.

Saints, remain faithful, be still, trust Him; He has
conquered your fight.

When you totally put all of your trust in Jesus
Christ,

The weeping, pain, disappointments, and suffering
will give you strong advice.

In this life of trouble, ups and downs, your face
will show some frowns.

I say, "Hold on and don't let go; you will surely
get your promised crown."

Questions

- Saints, will you continue to worship Him?
- Will you be a devoted witness for Jesus?
- Do you have a sincere passion for Him?
- When we have a passion for Jesus, our lives should

speak volumes. Does your life speak volumes?

- We should let our light shine for Jesus daily. How are you witnessing to the unbeliever?
- Does your life lead others to Jesus or away from Him?
- What will you do if Jesus calls your name today? Will you be ready?

"The Cry of a Pastor"

We heard pastors crying in the streets; they were
    really
saddened and hurt as they could be.

Tears were rolling down ever so hard, but they did
not want us to see.

There are so many pastors hurting inside and out.

They can't explain to anyone their spiritual
    drought.

Look around you and watch how their
    countenance changes.

Their pain is silent, and they are fighting hard; this
    ain't no game.

Yes, they know that Jesus cares for them, and He

has heard their cries.

But did you listen and see them give a big good bye?

Pastors are human just like you; they are not divine.

So many of them run very hard and are pressed for time.

When will the body of Christ see the pastors' true plight?

Sometimes, we wait too long—until they are gone out of sight.

At the conclusion of the matter, at the end of the day,

God is coming to take His true pastors away.

Their cries are going up to heaven on high.

Pastors are working hard to go to the place of "howdy howdy"

and never—"goodbye."

The burdens, joys, assignments, changes, charges, challenges, circumstances, consequences, and conditions of pastors and leaders will not be overlooked. God has heard the cries, concerns, crises, and clamor of pastors and leaders around the world. Today, we know that they are not alone, and help is available. Jesus came to my rescue and helped me, and He will help His pastors and His leaders today. The cries of pastors are real, and those cries will be attended to by the Lord of lords and the King of kings; His Name is Jesus.

The Bible tells us in Jeremiah 33:3, "Call unto me, and I will answer thee, and show thee great and mighty things, which thou knowest not." Pastors today are crying out to God more and more because these days are difficult and challenging. Pastors cry for their families, churches, communities, workplace, and so much more.

Ericka Anderson wrote an amazing and factual word. The word that she wrote states that

> pastoring is one of the most high-pressure jobs in the nation. According to the Soul Shepherding Institute, an organization that is organized to take care of the mental well-being of pastoral leadership, 90% of the pastors work 55–75 hours a week.[16]

In like manner, she writes that 75 percent of pastors report feeling "highly stressed" on any given week and that most pastors manage their family life with the much-needed attention. The pastoral care is demanding; some pastors have to work secular jobs as well as pastor their church; the workload is greater during the pandemic. Unending, unexpected, demanding, and stressful responsibilities sometimes get overwhelming. Pastors need a place of peace. There should be a room, a house, a golf course, a beach, a fishing pond, a vacation spot, or someplace where pastors can go and relax, rest, revive, renew themselves, and get replenished. Our pastors are overworked, and we must respond to their cries.

I hear the cries of pastors. Some people think that pastors only work on Sunday morning, but they work twenty-four seven some weeks. Pastors have to get up at all times of the night to answer the call of the pastoral ministry. Preaching the Word and teaching the Word are just parts of their responsibilities. Pastors have to do Christian counseling, assist the youth pastor, host conferences, hold ministry meetings, and officiate at funerals, weddings, and graveside services. Pastors visit the sick, those in prison, jail, hospitals, mental institutions, rehabilitation centers, and many other places. Pastors need a place of peace.

Do you hear the cries of some of the pastors? They need help like everyone else. Therefore, we need to pray for the pastors, give them good advice, encouragement, wise counsel, unconditional love, and seed offerings and gifts for just being valuable people in our lives. Pastors watch over your soul, and that is a huge responsibility. They need time for family, meditation, prayer, personal devotion, ministry, personal care, and recreation. Pastors and leaders must have a balanced life.

We will end this book by saying it's not too late for pastors, leaders, and laity to change and venture out from their comfort zones. Sometimes, your breakthrough comes in an unfamiliar place that God has ordained for you. Pastors and leaders, look out for each other and continue to be a blessing to your brothers and sisters in Christ.

"A Place of Peace"

A place of peace, pure, beautiful, and glorious
splendor.
Pastors and leaders, when was the last time you
really
relaxed? Do you remember?
Children, church, conferences, and company are
all in God's hands.
You can get away on that much-needed vacation
you planned.
Oh yes, the pressures of life can get pastors in a
mess.

The only way out of the dilemma is to call on
Jesus to bless.

Some people look at pastors as their gods.

Truly, pastors are just trying hard to do their
God-given part.

Don't worry, pastors and leaders: this, too, shall
pass.

There is a good old gospel song that says trouble
doesn't last.

Hold on, look up: your redemption draws nigh.

You don't have to worry; Jesus has heard your cry.

Keep on pressing your way and looking to the hill
of help.

Our dear and wonderful pastors, surely you will
be kept
by the Holy Spirit.

APPRECIATION

The women of God in this section are two of my mentors and prayer warriors who helped me when I was called to preach. They are my dear mother, late Rev. Cora Rebecca Crenshaw-Shuford, and my amazing sister, late Pastor Charlena Kay Shuford-Miller. God called them to their heavenly home; they are loved and missed dearly. Also, I honor my father, late Mr. Robert Lee Shuford, who left a legacy of love and leadership to our family. Moreover, I will never forget their labor of love, wisdom, prayers, encouragement, instructions, kindness, prophetic voices, and the anointing on their lives. They were awesome anointed jewels and great giants in the Lord. The world is a better place because of the indelible mark that they imparted in the earthly realm.

We thank our loved ones who have transitioned; we love them and miss them; we will see them again. Also, we remember my precious husband, late Bishop Frank T. Bozeman, and my brother-in-law, Rev. David Lee Grant, who went home to be with the Lord last year. They were men of honor, integrity, and loyalty, and they were anointed by God to preach the gospel.

These four preachers were awesome, anointed, prolific, prophetic, profound, and humble servants of God. Moreover, they were friends, prayer warriors, and devoted men and women of God.

NOTES

BIBLIOGRAPHY

The Message Bible, Peterson, Eugene, 1993.

Strong's Commentary, Strong, James 1890.

The New Strong's Complete Strong's Dictionary of Bible Words, Strong, James, 1880 and 1996.

Strong's Concordance, Strong, James, 1890.

Webster Dictionary, Webster, Noah, 1758–1843.

Why Can't Women Preach?, Bozeman Frank T., 2007.

The Power of Character in Leadership, Monroe, Myles, 2014.

Transform Your Thinking, Transform Your Life, Winston, Bill, 2008.

ABOUT THE AUTHOR

Bishop Hurdis Ophelia Shuford-Bozeman is a native of Elmore County, Wetumpka, Alabama. She graduated from Wetumpka High School with honors. Bishop Bozeman attended John M. Patterson State Technical College, Montgomery, Alabama, where she received her cosmetology diploma and cosmetology state teacher's license.

Bishop Bozeman continued her technical education and teacher's certification at Auburn University and Athens State University from 1984 to 1987. She was employed by Macon County public school systems for fifteen years. Bishop Bozeman received several teachers' awards at the county, district, and state levels. Moreover, she received the District Teacher of the Year award, District VICA Advisor of the Year, VICA State Leadership Team Member, and Outstanding Cosmetology Program in the state of Alabama.

In the fall of 1996, she retired from teaching in public schools. The bishop went into full-time ministry. Teaching and preaching God's Word became her first ministry after the ministry in the home. Bishop Bozeman has been in ministry as a licensed and ordained minister for thirty-seven years. She served as a senior pastor for nineteen years at

Global Word Fellowship, Inc., Montgomery, Alabama. In like manner, her husband, Bishop Frank T. Bozeman, was the presiding bishop of Global Word Fellowship.

Also, Bishop Bozeman served as the assistant pastor and senior pastor at Good Hope Missionary Baptist Church, Wetumpka, Alabama, for twenty-seven years. Therefore, she served in various areas of ministry for thirty-seven years.

She is a graduate of the following universities and colleges: Global Evangelical Christian College and Seminary (master of divinity and doctor of ministry), ICOF colleges and universities (doctor of Christian education), Summit University (doctor of ministry in Christian education and Christian counseling, the bachelor of arts in Christian education and Christian counseling).

She received several honorary doctoral degrees in ministry from various universities and colleges. Moreover, Bishop Hurdis Ophelia Shuford-Bozeman was born to Mr. Robert Lee Shuford and Rev. Cora Rebecca Crenshaw-Shuford.

Bishop Bozeman is the wife of Dr. Frank T. Bozeman. She is the first presiding bishop of Global Word Fellowship, Inc. and the founder of the Women Outreach Global International. She is the cofounder of Global Evangelical Accrediting Commission, Bozeman & Bozeman, Global Evangelical Christian College and Seminary, and the Global Word Fellowship, Inc.

Bishop Hurdis Bozeman is the mother of one biological daughter, Senior Pastor Colenthia Milner-Wright (Mr. David Wright). God also blessed Bishop Bozeman with a daughter, Sister Tammy Pearson, and two sons, Frank Tyrone II and Zacarius Justine Bozeman. She is the grandmother of six grandchildren: Jeremia, Destiny, Kendra, Dominique, Kendrick, and Aiden, and three great-grandchildren.

In closing: Dr. Hurdis Ophelia Shuford-Bozeman's motto is: "If I can get one soul saved, the cycle of saving souls will continue to go on and on." She is the author of five books: *Lord, Why Me?*, *Lord, Why Not Me? Storm after Storm*, *It's Personal*, *It's Personal 2*, *The Cry of a Pastor*.

Contact info: Bishop Hurdis Bozeman's email is hbozeman58@gmail.com

ENDNOTES

1   Jacqueline Ortega, *JustTestify* (Jacqueline Ortega, 2021), www.books.google.com/books?id=MSs1EAAAQ-BAJ.

2   C. S. Lewis, *The C. S. Lewis Bible: For Reading, Reflection, and Inspiration* (Grand Rapids, MI: Zondervan, 2021), www.books.google.com/books?id=9wYlEAAAQ-BAJ.

3   Lexico.com, s.v. "prayer," accessed April 8, 2022, www.lexico.com/en/definition/prayer.

4   Letha Barnes, *Master Educator* (Boston, MA: Cengage Learning, 2013), www.books.google.com/books?id=DMIZBQAAQBAJ.

5   Lexico.com, s.v. "insurrection," accessed April 8, 2022, www.lexico.com/en/definition/insurrection.

6   Lexico.com, s.v. "treason," accessed April 8, 2022, www.lexico.com/en/definition/treason.

7   Lexico.com, s.v. "rebellion," accessed April 8, 2022, www.lexico.com/en/definition/rebellion.

8   Mike Murdock□, as quoted in "Set Reasonable Deadlines," Emmandus Inspirational Network, blog, accessed April 8, 2022, http://www.emmanuelayeni.com/2016/02/set-reasonable-deadlines.html?m=1.

9   Lexico.com, s.v. "anoint," accessed April 8, 2022, www.lexico.com/en/definition/anoint.

10   Merriam-Webster.com Dictionary, s.v. "anoint," accessed April 25, 2022, https://www.merriam-webster.com/dictionary/anoint.

11   Merriam-Webster.com Dictionary, s.v. "peace," accessed April 8, 2022, www.merriam-webster.com/dictionary/peace.

12   Wikipedia, "Insight" entry, last modified on March, 3 2022, www.en.wikipedia.org/wiki/Insight.

13   Lexico.com, s.v. "increase," accessed April 27, 2022, www.lexico.com/en/definition/increase.

14   Barney Elliott Warren, "Joy Unspeakable," accessed April 8, 2022, www.hymnary.org/text/i_have_found_his_grace_is_all_complete.

15   Rick Warren (@RickWarren), "Much prayer, much power," Twitter, April 30, 2014, www.twitter.com/rickwarren/status/461511585270202368.

16   Ericka Andersen, "Why do pastors die by suicide?" ERLC, October 8, 2019, www.erlc.com/resource-library/articles/why-do-pastors-die-by-suicide.

CPSIA information can be obtained
at www.ICGtesting.com
Printed in the USA
BVHW072159230822
645288BV00013B/522